The JOHN DEE ORACLE

Wisdom from Queen Elizabeth's Magician

(INCLUDING A NEW TRANSLATION OF SIX ENOCHIAN CALLS BY JOHN MATTHEWS)

BY JOHN MATTHEWS,
WITH ART BY WIL KINGHAN

REDFeather™
MIND | BODY | SPIRIT
4880 Lower Valley Road, Atglen, PA 19310

Library of Congress Control Number: 2025930155

Designed by Alexa Harris
Cover design by Brenda McCallum
Type set in Ability Black/Map Roman/Baskerville

ISBN: 978-0-7643-6976-6
Printed in China

10 9 8 7 6 5 4 3 2 1

MIX
Paper | Supporting responsible forestry
FSC® C005748

Published by REDFeather Mind, Body, Spirit
An imprint of Schiffer Publishing, Ltd.
4880 Lower Valley Road
Atglen, PA 19310
Phone: (610) 593-1777; Fax: (610) 593-2002
Email: Info@redfeathermbs.com
Web: www.redfeathermbs.com

For our complete selection of fine books on this and related subjects, please visit our website at www.redfeathermbs.com. You may also write for a free catalog.

REDFeather Mind, Body, Spirit's titles are available at special discounts for bulk purchases for sales promotions or premiums. Special editions, including personalized covers, corporate imprints, and excerpts, can be created in large quantities for special needs. For more information, contact the publisher.

To Damon Albarn for inspiration,
Ari Berk for his wisdom,
and to the memory of John Dee and Edward Kelly
for sharing their vision.
—JM
Oxford, 2024

Contents

Dr John Dee:
BY ROYAL APPOINTMENT

BY CAITLÍN MATTHEWS

Her glittering majesty alights at Dee's own gate
To view the obsidian glass and contemplate
Her wayward fortunes in the reflective watchtowers
Of Enochian masters and planetary powers.

Serious divine, in deep respectful black,
His countenance steadfast, fearing neither the rack
Nor Walsingham's devises, for he guides her ships
To Atlantean shores where Gloriana never will be eclipsed.

He writes her royal warrant to Green—and Arctic lands,
Hails her "King Arthur's daughter," and these strands
Her rightful dower, by prior conquest won,
And her thin smile their dayspring's royal sun.

Her alchemist and shewstone of the body politick
Conjures a council more obedient than they who sit
About the privy table and abuse her graven patience
With husbands, wars, and treaties of two-faced alliance.

(Yet, should she once guess at those who, secret, come
To know what signs shall congregate, which deathly sum
Of hours and stars shall reckon up her reign's account,
Then she would cause her sad-faced necromancer to mount

The narrow scaffold's ladder and to dance the air
Unshriven, cut and quartered. But his prayer
Is loyalty's own gage, and all his conjurings
Are for her good advisance, her high aspirings.

Within his steady hand, he grasps the angelic key;
And by tablature of sigiled numerology,

Converses with eudaimonian companions
Within a skrying glass of archangelic pantheons.

His subtle navigations pass beyond shores seen and known,
Seeking the northwest passage to the heavenly throne;
To crave at the mercy seat a true philosophy,
To tincture all his works with golden alchemy.

Yet, his good works, the Queen's own Majesty requites
With golden favors; counts his offices as her delights,
Suffering none to check, control, molest her sapient
Diviner of the ways, whose charts disgorge from orient

To occident the jewels that deck her neck and sleeves.
Within her British earthly paradise, he receives
The mead of angels from his royal lady's hand,
Secret confessor, by appointment, to her fabled land.

Preface

John Dee's story reveals to us all that there will always be things we innately know exist without actually being able to prove they exist. —Damon Albarn, 2012

Over my desk is a portrait of Dr John Dee. It had been with me now for almost thirty years, and I still catch the doctor's eye—or maybe he catches mine—when I sit down to write. It's a comforting thought: that one of the truly great seers and visionaries who walked the earth should be somehow helping me in my own work.

Perhaps this is why devising and writing The John Dee Oracle often felt like a collaboration. As I read and reread the extraordinary notebooks and diaries he had left behind, I could almost feel him looking over my shoulder. Many of Dee's most important papers had miraculously survived in an old trunk, which lay unopened for years until its owners, who had bought it as furniture, discovered a hidden compartment containing manuscripts and letters. Now I felt I was on the track of my own treasure—the secret of Dee's magical system and the visions he so successfully and elaborately laid out in his writings.

The Oracle is the result of much pondering, meditation, and thought. Its final form was delivered to me as I sat enthralled, watching the first performance of the opera Dr Dee, created by Damon Albarn and Rufus Norris (on which my wife acted as an advisor), in which I saw the magical world of this great Elizabethan magus brought to life through astonishing music and amazing staging. I remain deeply indebted to Damon for this inspiration, which more than anything enabled me to complete this work, and for the wonderful quotation at the head of this page.

Thinking of the scene from the opera in which Queen Elizabeth I, in full panoply of costume and power, descends from the heavens onto the stage, as I prepared this new edition, I was inspired to add a new card: Gloriana, the magical name for she who was Dee's inspiration and whose power blessings now accompany each of the other cards. Her role as Queen over all readings brings a specific shift in the energy of the deck.

John Dee was a deep and complicated man, whose life and works are filled with magic. I suspect that he is not done with me yet, and that there may be more secrets to uncover. But for now, I am happy to present this revised and updated edition—retitled The John Dee Oracle—to an audience who will, I hope, receive some of that magic in their own lives.

—John Matthews
Oxford, 2024

• PART ONE •

The Story of Dr John Dee

I will lead you in the way of knowledge and understanding: and judgement and wisdom shall be upon you, and shall restored unto you: and you shall grow every day wise and mighty.

DIARY OF JOHN DEE, MAY 20, 1587

~ THE LIFE OF AN ELIZABETHAN MAGUS ~

Judged by any standard, Dr John Dee is a remarkable man. Mathematician, geographer, philosopher, visionary, alchemist, astrologer, historian—he is one of the most fascinating figures of the Elizabethan world. Yet, his extremely long life (eighty-one years) is filled with supposition, conflict, and mystery. To some he was a charlatan, to others a master. His knowledge of magic and arcane wisdom was second to none, and to this day his work continues to be read and studied by scientists, magicians, and mystics.

Born in London on July 13, 1527, into a family of Welsh origin, Dee's academic skills were recognised early in his life. He attended a Catholic grammar school, then went on to study at St John's College, Cambridge. There, his talents as a mathematician led to an appointment as one of the founding fellows of the newly established Trinity College. While still in his twenties, his reputation was already spreading beyond the shores of England, and he was invited to lecture at the University of Paris. At Trinity he made a name for himself by creating what may well be the earliest set of special effects for a production of Aristophanes's play *Peace*. For a scene in which one of the characters was required to fly up to heaven on the back of a scarab beetle, Dee created a full-sized model, which really did fly by means of pulleys and winches. The audience were so shocked and, in some cases, terrified that Dee was accused of sorcery—an accusation that was to follow him for the rest of his days.

Upon leaving Cambridge, Dee began the wandering life that was to be a recurring pattern for the rest of his life. Throughout the late 1540s and early 1550s, he travelled around Europe, studying for a time at Leuven, Brussels, and Antwerp. His reading was omnivorous, and it was at this time that he began a lifelong fascination with the mystical, including natural magic, alchemy, astrology, and astronomy.

Dee's lectures on algebra in the major universities of Europe were packed-out events, perhaps because he trod a fine line between mathematics and the occult interpretation of numbers. Throughout his life, Dee believed that numbers were the key to understanding the universe, and his mystical leanings fostered this.

At this time, he also met the famous mapmaker Gerardus Mercator. The two men became good friends, and when Dee returned to England in 1551, he brought with him a valuable collection of mathematical and astronomical instruments, including one of Mercator's globes. His interest in geography began at this time and would become particularly important later, during his years of service to Queen Elizabeth I. Back in England, Dee began to seek patronage—the only way for a man without a personal fortune to live the lifestyle he wanted and, above all, to purchase the books he needed for his studies. These were already beginning to form what would become one of the greatest libraries in Europe.

He now began to establish himself not only as a scholar but also as a notable astrologer. He attached himself to none other than William Cecil, later Lord Burghley, one of the most powerful men in the country, and through Cecil, he was introduced to King Edward VI. Dee presented the young king with two of his treatises, which earned him a gift of one hundred crowns—equivalent to more than £20,000 in today's currency—allowing him to purchase the living of the parish of Upton-upon-Severn. This brought in a stipend of eighty pounds a year, a considerable sum at the time.

Dee was very much an absentee vicar, remaining in London, where he was soon in great demand as an astrologer, casting horoscopes for both Queen Mary and Princess Elizabeth (soon to be queen). This quickly got him into trouble.

At the time, the church tolerated the use of astrology, providing it did not include any kind of magical actions and was based on pure mathematics, but someone must have reported that Dee's work went beyond this, because in 1555, he was arrested and charged initially with "conjuring" (another word for sorcery) and then with treason for having the temerity to cast a horoscope for Elizabeth.

How Dee managed to exonerate himself from this situation remains a mystery, since no transcripts of the trial have survived. It is known that he appeared before the Star Chamber and was subsequently examined by the Catholic bishop Bonner, Queen Mary's religious enforcer. Whatever passed between Dee and the bishop remains unknown, but it appears that Bonner recognized that Dee was a genuinely religious man and set him free. Throughout his life, Dee clung to his faith—although he was at one point ordained as a Catholic priest, he seems for the most part to have kept to the Protestant way. Even his most extreme magical operations were carried out invariably in the name of God, and the long period of communication with angels is a central aspect of this.

Everything changed in 1558, when Queen Mary died childless and was succeeded by Princess Elizabeth, daughter of Henry VIII and Anne Boleyn. Dee had become something of an unofficial tutor to the princess, through his connections with the powerful Northumberland family. Elizabeth must have liked and trusted the scholar, then in his thirties, because she requested that he consult the stars to find the most well-aspected date for her coronation. Dee chose January 15, 1559, and was almost certainly present at the coronation ceremony in Westminster Abbey. This connection is central to the inclusion of the extra card featuring Elizabeth herself, titled "Gloriana," the name by which she was known to her closest allies. With his position as occasional tutor and advisor to the queen ensuring him a regular income, Dee now embarked on a further round of travel, this time collecting books for his library. A rigorous journey—which took him first to Antwerp, then on to Zurich, Bratislava, Padua, Venice, and Rome—did not stop him writing, and by the time he returned to England in 1564, he had completed what is still regarded as his greatest work, the *Monas Hieroglyphica* (Hieroglyphic Monad). This is a detailed exploration of a glyph designed by Dee himself, which expressed the central tenets of an evolving magical system. Part Qabalah, part astrology, and part mathematics, with a touch of natural magic, it outlines the theory that all things are connected and interrelated. It lies at the heart of Dee's lifelong quest to discover the mystical unity of creation—a transcendent understanding of the divine forms that he believed underlay the visible world, which he called "pure verities." It is quite rightly pictured on the back of every card in the *Oracle*.

Upon his return to England, Dee began to explore two new avenues of knowledge. The first involved the geographical expansion of Queen Elizabeth's British Empire—a term Dee himself coined. He began advising the leading explorers of the time, providing maps and charts, many of which were at least partially imaginary, to help them claim more lands for the queen. At the same time, he worked his way through hundreds of supposedly historical documents, seeking evidence that lands once ruled over by Elizabeth's predecessors were still rightly hers. In 1577 he published *General and Rare Memorials Pertayning to the Perfect Arte of Navigation*, a work that set out his vision of a maritime empire and asserted English territorial claims over the New World. In a highly symbolic frontispiece, the book depicted the figure of Britannia kneeling by the shore, beseeching Queen Elizabeth to protect her empire by strengthening her navy.

This was followed in 1578 by *The Limits of the British Empire*, in which, using the twelfth-century pseudo-history *Historia Regum Britanniae* (History of the Kings of Britain) by Geoffrey of Monmouth, Dee argued that because King Arthur had supposedly extended his kingdom to include Ireland, Greenland, Iceland, and parts of the North Pole, so too might the queen. He argued also that England should garner new lands through colonization and that this vision could become reality by way of maritime supremacy.

By 1578, Dee had grown dissatisfied with pure learning as a means of uncovering the secrets of the universe. He then began to seriously explore the supernatural, employing several scryers or crystal gazers, whom he believed could communicate with angels.

This led to a fateful meeting that would forever change the course of Dee's life. His first medium, a man named Barnabus Saul, proved to be a fraud, but in March 1582, one of Dee's agents, a Mr. Clerkson, introduced him to a man who called himself Edward Talbot, who claimed to be one of the greatest mediums of his time. The real name of this man was Edward Kelly, as he revealed to Dee when he returned alone the next day. Many have written that Kelly was mad, or at least a fake who was after nothing other than money, but the truth is that, whether by accident or not, the material he brought to Dee was remarkable and, in many cases, extraordinarily accurate.

Dee was certainly convinced after a single session in which Kelly saw, in vision, the archangel Michael seated on a throne with a kneeling figure at his feet. When the figure, clad in robes of silk and crowned with laurel, rose and turned, his face was that of John Dee. Kelly joined the household at once.

Thus began one of the most famous partnerships of all time, which was to last, on and off, for almost five years. Every day the two men would set themselves up in Dee's darkened study in his house at Mortlake, on the outskirts of London, curtains drawn against the light reflecting from the Thames, and then, after reciting many prayers, Kelly would enter into a trance, the results of which Dee transcribed.

On June 20, 1584, Dee recorded a session in which Kelly experienced an extended vision, reportedly delivered by a feathered man, in which a magical glyph was described (see image below).

> *There appeared to him four very fair castles, standing in the four parts of the world: out of which he heard the sound of a trumpet. Out of every gate then issued one trumpeter, whose trumpets were of strange form, winged, and growing bigger and bigger toward the end. After the trumpeters followed three ensign bearers. After them six ancient men, with white beards and staves in their hands. Then followed a comely man, with very much apparel on his back. After him came five men carrying his train. Then followed one great cross, and about that four lesser crosses. After the crosses followed 16 white creatures. And after then, an infinite number seemed to issue, and to spread themselves orderly in a compass, almost before the foresaid castles.*

Later this vision was "expounded" by the spirit (or possibly another), as follows:

> *The four houses [castles] are the four angels of the earth. In each of these 4 houses, the chief watchman is a mighty prince, a mighty angel of the Lord, which hath under him five princes. The 24 older men are the 24 Seniors that St John remembereth. The 12 banners are the twelve names of God, that govern all the creatures upon the earth, visible and invisible, comprehending three, four and five. Out of these crosses come the angels of all the airs: which presently [at that time] give obedience to the will of men, when they see them.*

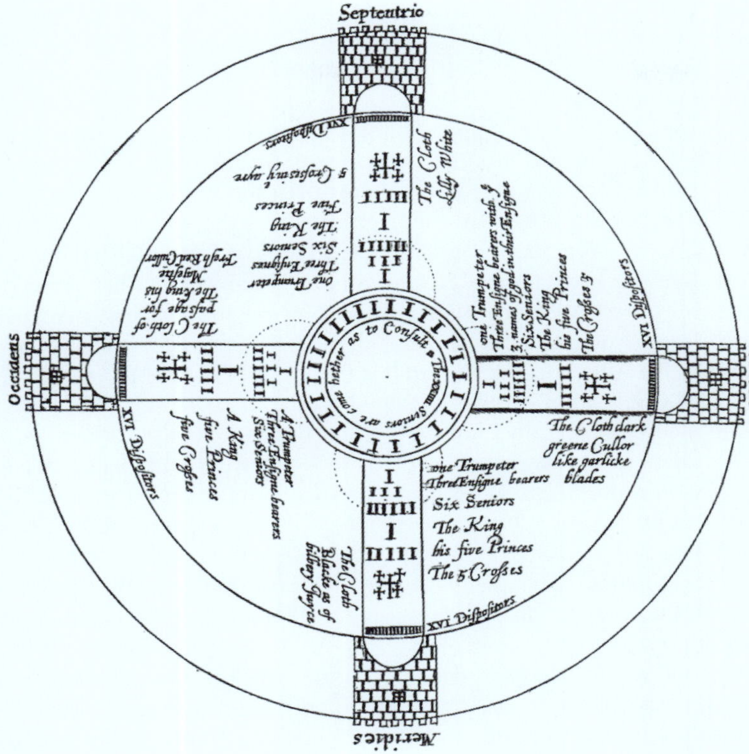

Dee's own depiction of the Talisman from *The True and Faithful Account of What Passed for Many Years Between Dr John Dee and Some Spirits*, 1659.

Opinions differ as to what happened next. It appears that Dee drew up the vision as shown here and that he subsequently ordered a copy to be inscribed onto a golden tablet. Because the version that has survived—and can still be seen in the British Museum in London—differs slightly from the version in Dee's notebooks, it has been suggested that the copy was made later, possibly at the behest of Meric Casaubon, who edited Dee's surviving manuscripts after his death. However, the essential content of the diagram, along with Kelly's delivery via the spirit, is the same, and it is this that generated the structure of *The John Dee Oracle*.

This is not the place to delve into the details of the magical correspondences, most of which have been derived in recent times from this diagram and from the even more complex Table of Earth, received by Kelly sometime later. Suffice it to say that the angel presences at the four directions, and the central point in which the magician stands to consult the spirits, convinced us that this could stand as the foundation for an oracle that invoked not only Dee's angelic correspondents but also the accumulated knowledge and wisdom of this remarkable man.

This was, however, only the beginning of the material that spewed forth from Kelly. Over the next months, the two men began to receive, record, and study an entire language, said to be no less than the original speech used by God to create the universe ("In the beginning was the Word, and the Word was with God"—Genesis 1:1) and later by Adam to converse with the Creator and the angels, and to name all the creatures of the earth. They referred to this language as Enochian, after the biblical patriarch Enoch, who was apparently the last human being to speak the language before its recovery by Dee and Kelly. After the Fall, Adam lost the use of this language and had to reconstruct a poor man's version, which became the basis for Hebrew.

The reception of Enochian had in fact begun a year earlier, on March 26, 1583, when Kelley first reported being shown a twenty-one-letter alphabet. A few days later he began to receive what became the *Liber Loagaeth* ("Book of Speeches from God"). It consists of forty-nine tables, arranged in squares of forty-nine letters. Each table is double sided, thus making ninety-eight pages (49 + 49) in all. The angels apparently never translated these texts, and they remain unclear to this day—despite the efforts of numerous students of magic to crack the code.

A second set of Enochian texts began to be received just after the vision of the Golden Talisman, and these came with English translations, which have enabled the partial understanding of Enochian. These are known as the *Claves Angelicae*, or "Angelic Keys," and Dee suggested that when used correctly, they could unlock the forty-nine gates of wisdom and understanding represented by the forty-nine tables. The language is obscure, to say the least, and still tests the mind of anyone trying to uncover its true meaning. Here is an example from the ninth key:

A mighty guard of fire, with two edged swords aflame . . .

Have settled their feet in the west . . .

These gather up the moss of the earth,

As the rich man doth his treasure . . .

In their eyes are millstones greater than the earth

And from their mouths rain seas of blood;

Their heads are covered with diamonds,

And upon their hands are marble sleeves.

In the same year that this was received, Dee met a visiting Polish nobleman named Albrecht Laski, who joined Dee and Kelly in their search for angelic wisdom. He seems to have been immensely impressed by the quality of what the two men were receiving, because he invited them to accompany him back to Poland.

Faced with the prospect of a wealthy patron and with some encouragement from the angels, Dee was persuaded to go, and in September 1583 they set out to make the long journey into Europe, accompanied by their families, servants, and an enormous baggage train containing some eight hundred books from Dee's library.

Unfortunately for Dee and Kelly, Laski turned out to be bankrupt and out of favor in his own country, and without their patron the two magicians were forced to adopt a nomadic life, travelling back and forth across central Europe, leaving their wives and children (and most of Dee's books) behind while the men sought audiences with several of the crowned heads of Europe.

Following unsuccessful interviews with Emperor Rudolf II in Prague and King Stefan Batory in Krakow, Dee briefly secured the patronage of a Bohemian nobleman named Vilem Rozmberk. But even he could not entirely protect Dee and Kelly from the reach of the church. Word of the presence of these notorious "magicians" reached Rome, and they were ordered to leave the Holy Roman Empire immediately. Several books in their possession were seized and burned, and fearing they might also face the flames, Dee and Kelly fled to Rozemberk's estates at Trebon, where they settled in relative comfort and resumed their angelic work. However, signs of a breakdown in the partnership—always uneasy due to Kelly's occasional outbursts of bizarre behavior—began to emerge. Dee attempted to use his son Arthur, then aged six, as a scryer, but this attempt failed. Matters finally came to a head in April 1587, when Kelly announced that the angels had told him that the two men must swap their wives.

It is an indication of the respect in which Dee held Kelly that he agreed to this (despite the tears shed by his wife, Jane), but only a few months later Kelly departed, vanishing into the mists of history and leaving behind numerous unpaid bills and a growing legend that had him still living in 1595, apparently serving as a mercenary in the war between Bohemia and the Turks.

Apparently deciding he had suffered enough on the Continent and beginning to feel the weight of his advancing years, Dee set out with his family on the epic return journey to England, which took nine months. He finally arrived back at Mortlake on November 23, 1589—only to discover that his house, left in the care of his brother-in-law, had been broken into and a number of his most-prized books and instruments stolen. He sought reparation and support from anyone who still favored him, including Queen Elizabeth, and was rewarded with the wardenship of Christ's College, Manchester.

This was far from the kind of position his intellectual abilities should have secured him, but many of the older courtiers who had supported him previously were dead or out of favor. It has been suggested that Dee received the cold shoulder because of a connection with the infamous School of Night, an atheistic circle founded by Sir Walter Raleigh and Henry Percy, the so-called Wizard Earl, who was suspected of necromancy. Dee may well have met

Christopher Marlowe at this time, and the playwright, who served as spy for Francis Walsingham, the head of Elizabeth's secret service, may have reported this to his master.

Dee's declining years are a record of misery. His time in Manchester seems to have been anything but happy. The fellows disliked him and saw him as a threat to their comfortable existence. At one point he advised on a case of seven children believed to be possessed of demons, but he seems to have taken little real interest in the matter. His second wife, Jane, died of the plague that ravaged Manchester, and in 1603 Queen Elizabeth died and James I became king. The new king was notoriously paranoid about witchcraft, penning a famous book on the subject, but in spite of this, Dee sent him a letter in which he claimed to be the new monarch's "sworn servant."

Dee likely returned to London around 1604 and settled in his house at Mortlake to live out his final days. His daughter Katherine, then twenty-three, moved in to care for him. Dee was now seventy-seven, an impressive age for that time, but despite occasional ill health, he seemed as lively as ever. He even planned another excursion to Europe, though it never happened, and resumed some rather vague angelic conversations with the assistance of Bartholomew Hickman, a scryer with whom Dee had briefly worked before Kelly's arrival. However, Hickman appears to have been primarily interested in exploiting Dee, and the records of these final workings soon petered out.

By this time, Dee was living in virtual poverty, forced to sell his prized books for food—a situation that must have been particularly painful for him. The last record we have of him is from 1608, where he crossed out the months in the almanac up until December, after which the entries stop. One final note, made by a friend of Dee's on March 26, 1609, features a death's head and the words "John. 3 a.m." According to the antiquary John Aubrey, writing several years later, Dee had accurately predicted the time and place of his own death.

This is the final note on the life of Dr John Dee, who, at eighty-one, was certainly one of the longest-lived men of his time. He was buried in the parish church of St. Mary the Virgin in Mortlake, though all traces of his grave have since disappeared.

John Dee's work and writings, which spanned decades, were truly extraordinary, but both his reputation and his contributions fell into disrepute for some time after his death. What remained of his great library was broken up or stolen soon afterward—most of it vanishing forever. About ten years later, the antiquary Robert Cotton, whose manuscript collection later formed the basis of the national archive now maintained by the British Library, purchased land around Dee's house and began digging, in the hope of uncovering some remnants of the old magician's work. He reportedly discovered several manuscripts and gave them to the scholar Meric Casaubon to edit and publish. The resulting book was the famous *A True & Faithful Relation of What Passed for Many Yeers Between Dr. John Dee (a Mathematician of Great Fame in Q. Eliz.*

and King James Their Reignes) and Some Spirits, which detailed Dee's workings with Edward Kelly.

To many people, this was the first they knew of Dee's angelic correspondences, and the book quickly sold out its first printing in 1659—despite the fact that the Puritan Commonwealth was still active. Unfortunately, Casaubon, who himself believed in the existence of spirits, declared in his introduction that when Dee thought he was communicating with angels, he was actually being controlled by evil spirits. This resulted in a general dismissal of Dee and his work for many years thereafter.

But John Dee was never completely forgotten, and over the years much of the tremendous legacy of his life has been uncovered. In the nineteenth century his work was discovered by the occult Order of the Golden Dawn, who claimed that their own esoteric work was directly inspired by Dee. Since then, he has become something of a figurehead among modern esoteric practitioners.

Most recently, we have seen the extraordinary opera *Dr Dee*, created by Damon Albarn and Rufus Norris. Performed onstage in Manchester, near Dee's old college, and at the Coliseum in London, it played to packed houses. Those familiar with Dee's work were moved by the portrayal of the great man's life and felt that something akin to a magical rite was performed onstage each night.

The power of Dee's work continues to inspire everyone who shares his belief in the magical wonder of the universe. The current *Oracle*, created in the spirit of Dr John Dee and drawing upon his writings, is intended as a tribute to his life and work as well as a practical means of discovering solutions to everyday problems and issues.

• PART TWO •

The Oracle and How It Works

Go forward . . . I will be thy guide

Thou shalt attain unto thy seeking . . .

The angels under my powers shall be at thy commandment.

(THE ANGEL MICHAEL TO JOHN DEE ON MARCH 11, 1582)

~ THE ORACLE DEVISED ~

An oracle is a magical device that enables the reading and interpretation of events in the past, present, and future. In Dr John Dee's time, everyone believed in the power of such magical devices and in the power of magic itself—whether through prayer, the invocation of holy angels and spirits, or the enactment of both simple and complex daily rituals. At every level of society, belief that spirits were everywhere, working invisibly for good or ill, was a perfectly acceptable idea and not in the least at odds with Christian belief. The efficacy of petitioning God, angels, or demons for help was widely accepted, and the search for and discovery of both physical and spiritual treasure through the use of magic was an everyday occurrence.

This was a time when Queen Elizabeth I practiced alchemy—she even possessed her own laboratory—and, like many others from all walks of life, sought the mystery of the Philosopher's Stone, said to transmute flesh into spirit and base metals into precious ores. Few made significant decisions without first consulting one of the many astrologers who advertised their services on nearly every street corner in the larger cities of Europe. Most people would have been entirely comfortable with the idea of an oracular device that could offer solutions both to everyday problems and matters of state.

Among the more popular methods of foretelling future events at this time was scrying, which involved looking for signs on or within any reflective surface—such as a metal plate, a basin of water, or even a polished thumbnail. Dee himself employed several expert scryers and owned a black mirror made from obsidian, into which he was said to often gaze, quickly falling into a trance. His companion, Edward Kelly, discovered that he could converse with angels by using this method.

The John Dee Oracle is based on the belief that we are surrounded by forces that can influence our daily lives. These can be seen to open doors that enable a deeper awareness of truths to which we are *already* privy but that, for whatever reason, we either ignore or discount. Thus, the *Oracle* is not a specifically magical device, but a means of calling to mind the things we need to access in order to enable us to solve problems. The simple truth is that we *all* are magical beings, whether we recognise it or not, and with the help of the *Oracle* we can access our own magical natures and discover the answers we seek.

This does not mean that the idea of helping spirits, angelic forces, and elemental influences should be dismissed. All of these are part of the inherently magical world we inhabit—we simply do not recognize or acknowledge their presence most of the time. When we sit down to use an oracle—whether Tarot, Lenormand, I Ching, or another—we open ourselves to an awareness of our own magical nature, as well as that of the cosmos around us.

The John Dee Oracle works on these profound, but simple, principles. The very act of taking the cards in your hands, of considering a question or issue for which you are seeking help, activates a deep magical power within you. It is a magical act and should be recognised as such. You may not initially be aware of the power of this action, but as you become more practiced in using the cards, you will find that your insights deepen—to the point where you will no longer need the meanings suggested in this book, which are, in any case, general and not meant to be considered as set in stone.

The *Oracle* combines a number of things: aspects of Dee's own life and work (he was a polymath whose interests embraced a vast range of topics), widely accepted magical practices of the time, and a variety of magical influences that can offer ways to interpret the events that profoundly affect our lives.

You will notice that all the cards feature the likenesses of people from the world of John Dee, or even older, and that most of them look directly out of the frame. This is to allow you to engage with the personalities who will offer you help and advice as you work with the *Oracle*. Look them in the eyes wherever you can, and feel their presence as invoked by the images.

In this new edition, we have added the *Gloriana* card, which features Dee's great patroness, Elizabeth I, Queen of England from 1558 to 1603. The queen was regarded as an almost mythical figure by those closest to her, particularly poets, musicians, courtiers, and sages such as Dee. Just as she ruled over the lives of her subjects, *Gloriana* now presides over readings with this oracle deck. Look for her presence in your readings and take note of the blessing she extends to every user.

~ THE CARDS AND THE TOWERS ~

Accompanying this book you will find a deck of twenty-eight cards and a foldout spread sheet based on a powerful talismanic image devised by Dr Dee himself (see p. 23). This is the central organising principle of the *Oracle* and illustrates how it works. It is based on a simplified version of the Talisman of the Golden Table, designed by Dee in 1584, following instructions received from the angels with whom he and his medium, Edward Kelly, interacted over a period of five years.

The talisman features four towers, one at each of the cardinal points of the compass, named as follows:

- NORTH: SEPTENTRIO
- EAST: ORIENS
- SOUTH: MERIDIENS
- WEST: OCCIDENS

The central point of the talisman represents the magical circle—often drawn in chalk or outlined in salt—within which the magician traditionally stood. The four towers correspond to the sacred directions, each holding a particular meaning. Additionally, these points are governed by specific angels, whose spheres of influence Dee and Kelly received through their dialogues with the angels.

For the purpose of the *Oracle*, we have slightly adapted the central point, originally designated as a place of consultation, to represent not only the Querent (the person asking the question) but the theme of Harmony, into which all the other elements of the circle flow. It is from this point that we are able to receive the blessing of understanding and to recognise the possible outcome of events with which we are currently concerned.

TOWER/POINT	DIRECTION	SPHERE
Oriens	(East)	Health/Well-Being
Meridiens	(South)	Intention/Direction
Occidens	(West)	Love/Inspiration
Septentrio	(North)	Work/Influences
Harmony	(Centre)	The Querent

These are the five principal positions on which the cards are laid; they interact with the meanings of the cards themselves to generate the *Oracle*.

The twenty-eight cards that form the deck are divided into four sets, each set numbering seven cards. Each set represents an aspect of Dee's life and interests, which also coincide with seven key aspects of an individual life journey.

THE ARCHETYPES

Magus	=	Knowledge
Alchemist	=	Transformation
Astronomer	=	Perception
Astrologer	=	Futures
Geographer	=	Journeys
Physician	=	Well-Being
Historian	=	The Map of Life

Each of the four sets is colour-coded and features an image that encapsulates the symbolic purpose of the individual archetype. The colours—Green, Red, Silver, and Gold—are inspired by the alchemical process, which Dee believed could transmute humble flesh into spiritual gold or base metals into precious ores.

According to where each card falls on the spread sheet, a different oracular meaning will be generated. These meanings are recorded below on pp. 24–25. Each aspect of the cards offers an oracle connected to the key subjects of health, work, love, and direction, according to the direction in which each card falls on the spread sheet. The card back depicts Dee's personal emblem, the Hieroglyphic Monad, which combines all his skills (see p. 99). A sample reading can be found on pp. 100–101.

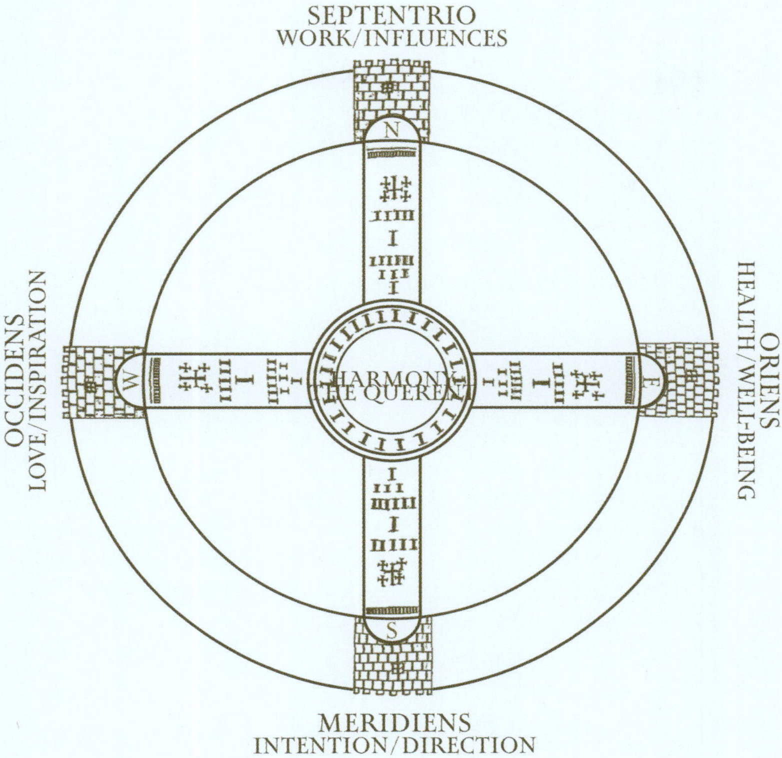

The Golden Talisman of Dr John Dee

~ THE ANGELS AND THEIR POWERS DECLARED ~

As shown above, the Towers represent four key aspects of life: **Health, Love, Work,** and **Intention/Direction**. Each is ruled over by a mighty archangel, who brings the appropriate wisdom, understanding, healing, or insight necessary to find a way through the storms and doldrums of life, as well as strengthening, supporting, inspiring, and healing us in every aspect of our lives.

Below you will find a brief account of the presiding angels, along with their planetary influence, colour, and element. Though not essential to the reading, each of these aspects can offer deeper significance when it comes to interpreting the message.

THE TOWER OF THE NORTH

The Angel of Septentrio: **URIEL**

Ruling over: Work

Planetary Influence: Uranus

Element: Earth

Colour: Green

Uriel, an angel particularly associated with literature and music, bestows upon us the gift of creative fire, as well as the power of prophecy. We appeal to him for the foresight of seeing into the future. Uriel is a minister of transformation and peace. He helps turn our worst disappointments into blessings. Overseeing us in our daily work, he brings strength and renewed energy, as well as new ways of seeing through any situation in which we find ourselves.

THE TOWER OF THE EAST

Angel of Oriens: **RAPHAEL**

Ruling over: Health

Planetary Influence: Mercury

Element: Air

Colour: Red

Raphael is the archangel of the planet Mercury. Known as a Harmonizer, he offers healing of all kinds and protects children, bringing guidance and sustenance to all who are lost, whether physically, emotionally, or spiritually. He can be invoked in matters of health, spiritual knowledge, and insight, and for help in navigating the concerns of daily life. Most importantly, he shows us how to share our spiritual insights with others.

THE TOWER OF THE SOUTH

The Angel of Meridiens: **MICHAEL**

Ruling over: Intention/Direction

Planetary Influence: Sun

Element: Fire

Colour: Gold

Michael is the archangel who rules the sun. As Initiator, he brings illumination and inspiration in many spheres of life through the efforts of our individual creative spirit. Michael is the guardian of all who stand alone with their unique vision for bettering the world and who refuse to compromise their ideals for the sake of money or fame. He can help us find and follow our deepest personal dreams.

THE TOWER OF THE WEST

The Angel of Occidens: **GABRIEL**

Ruling over: Love

Planetary Influence: Moon

Element: Water

Colour: Silver

Gabriel is the archangel who rules the moon. He brings increased spiritual awareness and shows the connection between soul and mind. He offers a deepening of spirituality within the family and work environment as well as personal relationships. He can be invoked for protection against inclement weather, for travel across water, for taking away sorrow, and for diminishing self-destructive tendencies while replacing them with the growth of new hope. When invoked in the area of love, he can help navigate the problems of relationships.

~ MAKING A READING ~

Shuffle the deck thoroughly while focusing on your question. Getting the question right is important, because the clearer and more thoughtful your question, the more distinct the answer will be. It's worth spending a little time to get it right. Avoid either/or or yes/no questions—for example, instead of asking, "Should I stay in this job or look for another?," ask, "What kind of job would be good for me?" or "What will help me move to another job?"

Once you have your question and have shuffled it into the deck, draw five cards, either from the top or randomly chosen, and lay them out face down as follows: Begin with the central position (Harmony) and turn this card over. This card represents you in the reading. Next, place the other four cards on each of the four Towers, starting at any point on the circle and then following the compass points in a sunwise direction—so if you begin in the south, the next card goes in the west, and so on.

Now, turn over the cards in the same order you laid them down, and consult the book for their meanings. If your question relates specifically to one of the subject areas—life/direction, work/influence, love/inspiration, or intention/beginnings—pay special attention to the card that falls on the corresponding tower. However, remember that the entire reading forms the answer, so consider all of the cards together.

If, after reading and considering the meanings of the five cards (and do not overlook the central card, since it often reveals aspects of your current situation that you may not have considered), you still feel the need for further clarification, you can select four additional cards and place them between the towers or cardinal points on the spread. This can provide a more rounded and complete reading, though the initial five cards are usually sufficient to provide an answer.

Each of the oracles of the four towers is accompanied by a question asked directly of you by one of the presiding angels. This constitutes angelic wisdom, which is evoked within you by the question. Answer as truthfully as you can, and consider the implications of both the question and your answer.

Just as a reigning monarch has long held the power to overturn rulings, such as orders for execution, in the *Oracle* we refer to the card representing Queen Elizabeth I (Gloriana) as "the Changing Card." This card has the ability to reverse the meaning of a reading and can be used in this way when it appears in a spread. If the Queen appears on any of the Towers, especially in the central position of Harmony, she offers the option to reverse the message of that position. The decision to do so rests with the reader. Even if the card does not appear when the cards are randomly drawn, include her Blessing as part of your interpretation of the answer.

• PART THREE •

The Oracle Cards Outlined

Then came Uriel to the man and took off that black hood . . . and then the man kneeled before Michael, and Michael dubbed him . . . with his sword. Then the man stood up. Then the man turned his face toward E[dward] *K*[elly] *the skryer. And the man did resemble me in countenance.*

—(DIARY OF JOHN DEE, MARCH 14, 1582)

1

The Magi

• KNOWLEDGE •

John Dee was, first and foremost, a magus—a person of great knowledge whose wisdom extends beyond the everyday. We might call him a magician, someone who understands that the world does not end at the limits of the senses but reaches further into the realm of the spirit. Dee himself claimed to have received much of his wisdom from angels, and some of his most powerful and compelling writings are those in which he documented the hundreds of hours spent, through his medium Edward Kelly, discussing a wide range of subjects and receiving detailed, often astonishing, responses from his angelic communicators.

Few of us can do this, or would seek to do so if we could, but we are all, at some time and in some way, aware of things for which we can find no rational explanation. We do not have to encounter a spirit, or a faery being, or an elemental in order to believe in them; neither is such a belief necessary to understand the influence that things out of this world can have upon us.

In *The John Dee Oracle*, the figure of the mage and philosopher represents wisdom and knowledge, which are often very different and can originate in ways that are neither quantifiable nor qualifiable. In daily life, this type of wisdom is instinctual; it is best described as "knowing without knowing"—an intuitive understanding that may relate to a particular issue or problem. When one of the four magi (represented here by four of the most famous magicians) appears in your reading, their wisdom and knowledge will apply to your issue at the most profound and mysterious level.

Green Magus

JOHN DEE

Oracle of the West

(LOVE/INSPIRATION)

When love or inspiration falter, look to the deepest levels of awareness. Ask yourself what your true motives are and what purpose is best served by choosing one course of action over another. In relationships, seek to understand the real nature of your motivation—are you selfishly holding on to a relationship that has run its course, or are you seeking change for purely self-centred reasons? Consider the real influence and inspiration that moves you though life and truly make you happy without qualification.

Gabriel asks:

Whom do you serve with an open heart?

The Green Magus is represented by Dee himself, in his role as prophet and seer to Queen Elizabeth I, and as someone seeking wisdom outside the sphere of the physical world. Wherever he looks, he seeks to understand where spirit meets the physical. His great desire is to read the code of the cosmos, to see where linked truths form a chain of understanding and realization. His many disciplines all lead back to this idea. Within the *Oracle* he points to inner meanings inherent within any situation.

Oracle of the North

(WORK/LIVING)

No matter what problems arise at your workplace, there are always ways to resolve them. These solutions may range from the extreme of moving on to the simple choice of doing nothing. However, it is essential to examine every aspect from as many perspectives as possible to ensure you have the most complete understanding of the situation. The same principle applies if you are engaged in creative work. Avoid getting bogged down in the details; instead, seek a vantage point from which you can view all directions.

Uriel asks:
What is the heart of your work?

Oracle of the Centre

(GENERAL/PERSONAL)

When you least expect it, wisdom may spring from the earth at your feet. You should always be aware of the invisible influences that surround you and can affect you in every walk of life. Do not consider just the hard facts that you can measure with your senses, but look to the small signs that are everywhere you look.

Oracle of the South

(INTENTION/DIRECTION)

What direction are you really seeking? Do you understand what you have undertaken or are about to undertake? If you set out on a journey or take a course of action without forethought, do not be surprised if things take unexpected turns. For some this is a natural way; for others a more moderate and considered course is more appropriate. Whatever way you choose to go, be aware that help is always at hand, and do not refuse offers of support if they are offered with good intent.

Michael asks:
What is the mainspring of your motivation?

Oracle of the East

(HEALTH/WELL-BEING)

Everyone is prone to go out of balance from time to time, and this can result in sickness or depression. Look for places where your life seems less balanced and overwhelmed, and do not be afraid to seek advice. Take care before you undertake things that might overwhelm the body. Be aware of your limitations before you accept a challenge that could cause you to suffer ill health. Always remember to give yourself time to rest and recuperate when the going gets tough.

Raphael asks:
What comfort sustains you?

Gloriana's Blessing

To you I give the power of understanding. Not only of the world but of your own most secret and profound desires. Bring all that you are to your life, and you shall reap its rewards.

Red Magus

EDWARD KELLY

Oracle of the West

(LOVE/INSPIRATION)

Sometimes, those you trust and care for can betray you. While this may not be intentional, it can still harm your relationships on many levels. It's important to be as honest as possible with those close to you. Family ties are immensely valuable to all of us, and we should do everything we can to nurture them and recognize their importance. When seeking inspiration from others, remember that you, too, can inspire those around you.

Gabriel asks:

How long does the flame of love and inspiration burn?

The Red Magus is represented by Edward Kelly, Dr Dee's medium and amanuensis for many years. Little is known about Kelly's early life. He suddenly appeared in 1582 and quickly became indispensable to Dee by claiming the ability to communicate with angels. While many have assumed he was a charlatan, and certain aspects of his life do not hold up to scrutiny, there is evidence suggesting he was a genuinely skilled medium. Here he is shown scrying into a crystal ball prior to giving voice to angelic wisdom.

Oracle of the North

(WORK/LIVING)

Every aspect of life can have more than one interpretation—some with many. Be cautious not to jump to conclusions or attempt to understand events too quickly. Evaluate what is truly valuable to you both in work and life, and avoid being distracted by too many potential courses of action. Focusing on one part of the journey will often illuminate others.

Uriel asks:
What is really valuable to you?

Oracle of the Centre

(GENERAL/PERSONAL)

Even though you believe you have reached a turning point in your life, there may still be surprises in store for you. Always try to be ready for sudden and unexpected twists of fortune, which may leave you floundering for a while but actually open new directions in your life. A rigid and uncompromising approach toward everything generally ends by putting you in a cul-de-sac. Try to put aside feelings of anger or despair, which only obscure your vision. Listen to your inner voice, which is often wiser than the one with which you address the world.

Oracle of the East

(HEALTH/WELL-BEING)

If you are one of those people who possess great drive and energy, remember to give yourself time off every now and then. Constant running wears out even the strongest engine, and occasional maintenance can do wonders. It is very important to take time out for enjoyment. Everyday simple pleasures can be overlooked when we are under pressure. Try easing off for a day or so and you will find that your health issues either settle or clarify.

Raphael asks:
When did you last take a proper vacation?

Oracle of the South

(INTENTION/DIRECTION)

Sometimes, you can get lost in the details of a situation and suddenly find yourself with too many possible directions to take. In such moments, it's important to step back and take time to consider the true nature of the problem before you. Can you seek the opinions of others, or do you always insist on finding the answer yourself? If you are determined and idealistic, be cautious not to become too absorbed in the issue—at least until you have considered every aspect.

Michael asks:
Do you truly know in what direction you are headed?

Gloriana's Blessing

I offer you the power of forethought. May you always remember what lies behind and before you, and make your choices in alignment with the needs of the moment. Fear not, for if you are aware of your true path, you cannot fail.

Gold Magus

JOHANNES FAUSTUS

Oracle of the West

(LOVE/INSPIRATION)

Your own innate wisdom can often tell you if you are ill matched in love. Do you listen to such inner promptings or allow yourself to fall in love despite them? It is always wise to look carefully at the true nature of a relationship before moving to a deeper level. Similarly, in terms of inspiration, there can be many glamorous and attractive people and things that fill you with the desire to emulate them. Be careful of this, since it can lead you to stretch beyond your limits.

Gabriel asks:

Is the path you have chosen really the right one?

The Gold Magus is represented by Johannes Faustus, the celebrated magician who may or may not have been a real person. His story is told in the eponymous poem by Johann Wolfgang von Goethe (1749–1832). In it, he makes a pact with the Devil to give him extended life and to bring before him the spirit of Helen of Troy, with whom he is in love. He becomes the most powerful magician of his age and is saved in the end by his innate goodness. He is particularly powerful in the area of ancestral wisdom, looking into the deepest places for answers both to present and future events.

Oracle of the North

(WORK/LIVING)

Being true to your vision is of paramount importance both in the work you do and the life you live. While not all of us are fortunate enough to fulfill our dreams, we should at least strive with every fiber of our being to do so. However, we must also learn to manage disappointment, which can seriously undermine all aspects of life. If the defeats that sometimes accompany daily existence are allowed to take precedence, their accumulation will work against you over time. Be mindful of this and do all you can to address such matters as they arise.

Uriel asks:
Where do you turn for help when everything seems to go wrong?

Oracle of the Centre

(GENERAL/PERSONAL)

I invite you to look within and consider the deepest aspects of your life and the situations that arise. Do these events repeat themselves in your life? Are you following the same pattern over and over? Everyone possesses innate wisdom that helps us avoid traps and pitfalls. When faced with difficult circumstances, carefully examine whether this issue has arisen before. If it has, you need to identify its origin and address it. Remember that some problems may have roots in the past. Connections with older family members might need to be evaluated to understand the repetition of certain patterns.

Oracle of the South

(INTENTION/DIRECTION)

Ask yourself every day: Where are you going? Where are you on your journey? Is anything blocking you? If so, what is the source of this blockage? If your intention is clear—both to yourself and to others—you will encounter much less opposition. Strive to be honest with yourself in everything you intend to do. Are your goals realistic? How long will it take to achieve them? With these factors clearly mapped out, your life compass will hold true, and the path to achievement will be that much clearer.

Michael asks:
Are you being honest with yourself?

Oracle of the East

(HEALTH/WELL-BEING)

Every aspect of life has its checks and balances, health no less than others. There will be moments when you feel on top of the world, and others when you feel that just getting out of bed is too much for you. When this happens, you need to look for patterns in your life. Are you pushing yourself too hard? Are others laying too much of a load upon you? What circumstances recur at the times when you feel drawn toward other states of being? Be kind to yourself at every opportunity, though not at the expense of others.

Raphael asks:
Are you being too considerate for your own good?

Gloriana's Blessing

I offer you the blessing of honesty. Consider all that is happening in your life and see that it is just and honest and right for those around you. Know your own worth, and you shall make the decisions you need to make.

Silver Magus

MERLIN

Oracle of the West

(LOVE/INSPIRATION)

Relationships are seldom equal, and in many cases one or other of the people involved will be the dominant partner. While this can work well, especially if one person is comfortable with a lesser role in the relationship, the imbalance can cause a breakdown in the relationship, which can become permanent. Look for a more balanced and sustainable way of working together as equals and allow yourselves to be an inspiration for each other.

Gabriel asks:

Who will lead the way to harmony?

The Silver Magus is represented by the figure of Merlin, perhaps the most famous magus of all time. Here he is seen with his great love, Nimuë. Though generally considered to be a fictional character associated with the legends of King Arthur, under the name Myrddin he is acknowledged to have been an actual historical prince in sixth-century Wales. His knowledge of the natural world as well as the stars and planets makes him a valuable guide to discovering the deeper wisdom needed for many issues.

Oracle of the North

(WORK/LIVING)

Whatever work you do tends to require subtlety and an awareness of things left unsaid. Your ability to read between the lines is a powerful skill, though it can occasionally make life difficult, since people may see you as a negative force. In life, as in work, your skill manifests in your ability to read people and acknowledge them in a deeply personal way. At times you may seem almost magus-like, but in reality, this is simply the product of sensitivity to the needs of others and a way of seeing past surface conditions to the heart of any matter.

Uriel asks:
What truly lies beneath the surface of life?

Oracle of the Centre

(GENERAL/PERSONAL)

Be aware of the great potential you hold, for just as strength existed in the young Arthur, so it may exist within you. Focus on the strengths you possess, and never turn away from them because of circumstances beyond your control that seem to work against you. Look deeply into your reasoning for each decision, and address the aspects that seem weakest—the strong will take care of themselves. Also, look to the stars that rise and set above you.

Oracle of the South

(INTENTION/DIRECTION)

Recognising the true direction in which you want to move can sometimes be harder than expected. You may find yourself travelling a road you would rather avoid, but it can be difficult to switch direction, especially later in life. However, your innate abilities of perception and balance are such that, if you take the time to carefully consider your options, you may find the road before you opening up, with previously unacknowledged or unseen paths branching off into fresher pastures.

Michael asks:
How did you come to be on this path?

Oracle of the East

(HEALTH/WELL-BEING)

At some point you may be forced to acknowledge your own shortcomings and limitations. This can have a powerful effect both at a physical and spiritual level. If you find yourself faced with feelings of doubt and uncertainty, or with previously unacknowledged health issues, consider whether there are unrecognised aspects in your life that are blocking you and causing stress and dissatisfaction. An acknowledgement of these things can often result in a new wave of confidence and a more secure attitude to health and well-being.

Raphael asks:
Where is your true centre?

Gloriana's Blessing

I offer you the blessing of inner vision. You may perceive the truth of situations and find your way to the answers you seek. Trust your own wisdom and align it with others.

2

The Alchemists

• TRANSFORMATION •

Alchemy was regarded as an immensely important and serious discipline in Dee's time. Any self-respecting scholar seeking to understand how creation worked would have studied the numerous books on the subject. Dee's library is known to have contained several hundred volumes on alchemical work, and he himself studied it extensively. Like many other monarchs of the sixteenth century, Queen Elizabeth I had her own laboratory, and Dee undoubtedly carried out many experiments both at her behest and for his own interests. Alchemy is essentially a proto-science that would later evolve into chemistry. Even the highly respected scientist Isaac Newton began as an alchemist, filling countless notebooks with his findings.

There were essentially two kinds of alchemy: physical and spiritual. The latter is often overlooked in favour of the more sensational history of the former, which focused on the transmutation of base metals such as lead or tin into gold and silver. This work centred on the creation of the Philosopher's Stone, believed to possess the power not only to transform base elements but also to extend human life indefinitely. The spiritual aspect of the science, however, was concerned with the transformation of the soul to a higher level, and alchemical laboratories were often located near chapels or oratories.

Only a person of great personal goodness was expected to succeed in conducting alchemical experiments. In 1583, Edward Kelly brought forth a scroll he claimed to have found in a tomb, which contained what appeared to be a map identifying sites where treasure was hidden. In addition, he brought a small amount of "red powder," which he claimed (and Dee believed) to be from the Philosopher's Stone. No one knows what became of this powder or whether it was genuine, although those who saw it at the time swore it produced as much as 22,000 pounds of gold!

In the context of the *Oracle*, the alchemists are primarily concerned with personal transformation and point the way toward methods by which this can be achieved. As with each set of cards, Dee himself is featured, along with three other famous practitioners of the high art.

Green Alchemist

NICOLAS FLAMEL

Oracle of the West

(LOVE/INSPIRATION)

The changes brought about by love are not always good for us. There can be times when our stars are mismatched, and it is wise to recognise this from the outset and proceed with caution. Inspiration, too, can be misleading, but when the energy it ignites within us is constant, it transforms us at the deepest possible level. Wherever you turn for love and inspiration, be mindful of your true motives.

Gabriel asks:

Where do you look first for meaning and inspiration?

The Green Alchemist is represented by Nicolas Flamel, one of the most famous practitioners of proto-science in the West (1330–1418). After purchasing a mysterious twenty-one-page book written by the semilegendary Abramelin the Mage, Flamel and his wife, Perenell, worked together to create the Philosopher's Stone, which was believed to grant them immortality. A gravestone dating from 1418 resides in the Musée de Cluny in Paris, but some claim that this was a hoax and that Flamel is, in fact, still alive. His mastery of the secrets of alchemy makes his oracles invaluable in all matters of personal transformation.

Oracle of the North

(WORK/LIVING)

You may need to transform your life and work at any time. Be ready for this if necessary. Sometimes as we move though life, we reach turning points that necessitate letting go of old worn-out conditions and directions. If challenges occur that suggest a need for change, be prepared to be fluid rather than digging in your heels.

Uriel asks:
How do you react to opposition in your life?

Oracle of the Centre

(GENERAL/PERSONAL)

Everyone must transform themselves at least once in their lifetime. Indeed, it can be said that we transform ourselves daily as we make many decisions, both great and small, on our journey through life. This should be recognised, acknowledged, and honoured—be aware of each moment as a potential turning point. Actively look for the changes in direction that can transform your life. It has been wisely said, "That which does not transform is not living." Be wary of becoming too settled in your ways, and learn to approach challenges with a quiet heart.

Oracle of the South

(INTENTION/DIRECTION)

No matter how familiar a road may seem, you can still get lost. Always watch for signposts and stay alert to the messages they offer. These signs are often not obvious at first glance, so observe carefully. The broadest way may not always be the right one for you; consider the less trodden path if it feels right. Wherever your path leads, be willing to accept help and advice when it is well intentioned.

Michael asks:
How often do you look for, or recognise, signposts?

Oracle of the East

(HEALTH/WELL-BEING)

The movement from health to sickness and from sickness to health is a subtle one. Sometimes we are unaware of the signs we should be looking for. It is wise to be attentive to stress, anxiety, and exhaustion, since these may lead to more-serious illness. As with most matters of life, health and well-being are very much a matter of balance. Pay attention to any signs of imbalance and look to ways of dealing with this.

Raphael asks:
Is your life is weighted more in one direction than another?

Gloriana's Blessing

The blessing I give is one of self-awareness. Allow every moment that passes to be filled with strength and joy. Remember who you are and what gifts you possess.

Red Alchemist

JOHN DEE

Oracle of the West

(LOVE/INSPIRATION)

Relationships should always be built on integrity, honesty, and truth. If you find yourself in a situation where none of these things are in evidence, take care. In the same way, remember that the things that inspire you may not always be right for you. Consider the true origins of such inspiration and if they really do reflect the ideas you think they do. Look for ideas that transform you from ordinary to extraordinary.

Gabriel asks:

How do you know when something inspires you?

The Red Alchemist is represented by Dee himself. This aspect of his life was immensely important to him, and he devoted a great deal of time to working on this profoundly complex material. After Edward Kelly's arrival in 1583, Dee's alchemical work took on even greater significance, since Kelly claimed to have discovered a mysterious red powder derived from the Philosopher's Stone—the greatest prize in the practice of alchemy. Dee appears to have been convinced of the powder's power, since it is frequently mentioned in his diaries and other writings. Through Kelly, Dee discussed the powder with various angelic presences and was told that it was part of God's medicine for the elevation of humanity.

Oracle of the North

(WORK/LIVING)

Passionate belief can drive us onward and supply us with the impetus to carry out the tasks we need to accomplish, but sometimes it can falter when least expected, leaving us stranded. Try to balance belief in yourself or your ideas with a dose of reality. Remember that sometimes the most attractive-looking package can contain things you are not be prepared for. Look for ways to transform yourself and your ideas when necessary.

Uriel asks:

What kind of change in circumstances would you contemplate?

Oracle of the Centre

(GENERAL/PERSONAL)

Though you may strive as hard as possible and sometimes seem never to progress, you need to learn how best to work though the checks and balances of daily life. If you are feeling stuck, consider what inspiration you may seek to help you push through the blockage. Spiritual disciplines can help, but beware of relying too heavily on the words and thoughts of others. Be strong in yourself and concentrate on what stimulates you. Even opposition can become a force to drive you forward.

Oracle of the East

(HEALTH/WELL-BEING)

Recovery after illness or receiving a shock may take longer than expected. Do not rush back to work or resume normal daily life; instead, take the time to reflect on every aspect of what you do and how you live. You may find it necessary to reassess your lifestyle and seek new ways to grow and learn. Whatever your concerns, remember that a solution can often be found—sometimes in the most unlikely places.

Raphael asks:

Are you open to discovering new vistas in your life?

Oracle of the South

(INTENTION/DIRECTION)

Wherever your journey takes you, consider every aspect as a way of learning more. If you travel to other countries, take the opportunity to learn about their culture. If you are a traveller of the imagination, be as open as you can to ideas that are foreign to you, and remember that no knowledge is wasted. Look to the rarest and most-wonderful sources for inspiration.

Michael asks:

Where does your imagination carry you?

Gloriana's Blessing

My blessing to you is of energy—that you may discover the fountain of strength within yourself and learn to work with it. Thus will your life move forward with greater ease and insight.

Gold Alchemist

ROGER BACON

Oracle of the West

(LOVE/INSPIRATION)

Wherever love or inspiration strikes, it is easy to become swept up in the maelstrom of emotions. However, remember that the future also requires planning, and consider the demands that family life can bring. Plan ahead, but do not allow yourself to become overly obsessed with security—freedom is important too. As with everything, you can transform your fears into strengths and your dreams into reality.

Gabriel asks:
What gives you the greatest sense of freedom?

The Gold Alchemist is represented by Roger Bacon (1214–94), one of the earliest Western scholars to study alchemy. His extensive learning and the mysterious nature of much of his work earned him the title "Doctor Mirabilis." Bacon is often described as one of the first early scientists to use a proper scientific method, and his criticisms of the church's teachings on the natural order of the universe led to his imprisonment on several occasions. He is also known to have practised alchemy, exploring the mysteries of transformation to build a greater understanding of the workings of the universe. Additionally, he is said to have created a brass head that uttered prophecies at his command. Within the *Oracle*, his role is that of guide and master of inner truths.

Oracle of the North

(WORK/LIVING)

It is important to plan for the future, to be prepared for all eventualities. If you do not want life to surprise you, consider your options before beginning any new project. Remain aware of the levels of commitment required by any task, domestic or professional. Do not overburden yourself, but try to balance work and play in equal measure. Be sure you are well grounded before you seek to roam the shores of the imagination too frequently.

Uriel asks:

What plans would you like to implement now?

Oracle of the Centre

(GENERAL/PERSONAL)

Consider how you may transform your life from within. Circumstances often persuade us that we must live according to the patterns of the time, but all too often we do this at the expense of our inner life. The wise person will contemplate the strength or weakness of the spiritual self and look for ways and means of helping the inner flame shine through. Keeping in touch with your inner self is every bit as important as being connected to the outer world. Neither should dominate, but rather be harmonious.

Oracle of the South

(INTENTION/DIRECTION)

No matter how determined you are, you may sometimes find yourself on a different path than the one you expected or desired to follow. This does not mean you are helpless or must always stick to the life you seem prepared for. Be mindful of where best to focus your energies, and consider your goals at every junction. Whenever possible, continue on the path you are on until you can see where it leads. Your journey will bring transformation into your life. Be sure you are prepared for this before setting forth.

Michael asks:

Can you be guided by the thoughts of others?

Oracle of the East

(HEALTH/WELL-BEING)

Life can take you in many different directions—not always the ones you would prefer. Such abrupt changes can cause stresses that are difficult to manage. This can be alleviated by staying alert to unexpected turns and being as prepared as possible for them. If you cannot do this, seek the support of friends, both inner and outer, to help you until you reach calmer waters.

Raphael asks:

Who or what gives you the greatest degree of support in crisis?

Gloriana's Blessing

My blessing to you is that you learn to see ahead through even the darkest moments, to recognise and acknowledge the help that is at hand, and the will to accept it when needed.

Silver Alchemist

RAYMOND LULL

Oracle of the West

(LOVE/INSPIRATION)

Look to your greatest point of inspiration and set your compass by it. Don't allow criticisms or bad advice to rule your life. Remember that partnerships should be mutually supportive, and that if one or other takes the lead, this should be for only as long as necessary before returning to mutual harmony. Try to pull your weight equally without trying to be dominant. Be supportive, but do not overwhelm.

Gabriel asks:

What is the point of balance in your relationship?

The Silver Alchemist is represented by the powerful figure of Raymond Lull (1232–1315), a Majorcan writer, monk, philosopher, and reputed magician. Today, he is regarded as one of the pioneers of computer theory. He lived a wandering life, and although he married young, he later became a Franciscan monk. With access to several extensive monastic libraries, he wrote treatises on alchemy, botany, and what may be the first European novel, *Blanquerna*. He also learned Arabic and studied books written in that language. His passion for alchemy exposed him to the risk of persecution, but his saintly demeanour spared him from the church's attention. As a character in the *Oracle*, he brings a gentle wisdom to the alchemy of the soul.

Oracle of the North

(WORK/LIVING)

Dreams convey messages that you may or may not choose to hear. They can suggest deeply buried concerns that you are neglecting, pointing you toward ways that can offer regeneration and clarity even in the worst situations. As you move through life, pay attention to the hints and clues that may come from the most unlikely places or people.

Uriel asks:
Do you pay attention to your dreams?

Oracle of the Centre

(GENERAL/PERSONAL)

Do not allow yourself to become too dependent on the five senses, on what you perceive as reality. Look to the realm of the imagination also, and especially to the idea of magic. It is all too easy to be caught up in the manifestation of the outer world and to neglect the secret universe that surrounds us all. Don't just depend on your everyday understanding, but look at the world from the inside as well as the outer.

Oracle of the South

(INTENTION/DIRECTION)

Do not let yourself be deflected from your true path. When times seem harsh, it is all too easy to feel the need to seek a less conflicting or stressful path. It is better in the long term to keep focused on your original vision and to do all that you can to remain faithful to it. You have a great deal to offer, and if you remain steadfast, you will discover ways to deal with even the most difficult situation.

Michael asks:
Where can you be true to yourself?

Oracle of the East

(HEALTH/WELL-BEING)

Be careful of getting caught up too much in a particular situation rather than seeking the best solution. Always look to the most important place of strength and inspiration in your life, and remember that if you neglect the roots that nourish you, illness and imbalances may follow. Be as kind to yourself as you are to those around you, and you will find untapped reservoirs of energy.

Raphael asks:
How can you best transform the world around you?

Gloriana's Blessing

My blessing to you is that you observe all the wonders around you: the strength of the natural world, the beauty and power of the animal kingdom, the birds of the air, and the creatures of the ocean. All of these offer strength and energy when you need it.

3

The Astronomers

• PERCEPTION •

The function of astronomy in the Elizabethan world stretched a great deal further than the study of the heavens and the measuring of stars and planets. Rather, it had much more to do with the influence of these heavenly bodies on the world. In this, astronomy remained a partner of astrology, though Dee seems always to have distinguished between the two disciplines, while acknowledging their connection. Dee himself took thousands of readings of the positions of stars and planets and, from them, devised complex calculations regarding the effects of their movement and relationship one to the other. When a supernova was observed in the constellation of Cassiopeia in 1572, Dee believed that it was a portent of great things to come. In particular, he thought it heralded the imminent discovery, perhaps by himself, of the Philosopher's Stone—the greatest prize sought by the alchemist and the magician at the time. Above all, Dee believed that if he could learn to read the positions of the heavenly bodies, he would be closer to cracking the code of creation. Though he had virtually no understanding of the vastness of the cosmos, or the tides that governed it, he intuitively grasped that by measuring the endlessly changing planisphere, he could unlock a vast chamber of secrets. Despite the comparatively primitive nature of the telescopes then in existence, Dee was aware of the existence of over a thousand stars. Within the scope of the *Oracle*, the Astronomers are dedicated to perception, to observing the effect of one aspect of life, the actions of an individual, and the expression of one source of energy upon each other. They can help us recognise the importance of such influences and remind us to be aware of them at moments of decision or change.

Green Astronomer

NICOLAUS COPERNICUS

Oracle of the West

(LOVE/INSPIRATION)

Inspiration clings to you—but are you making it welcome? It is all too easy to find yourself caught up in a situation where your ideas are drained of meaning and strength by outside forces. Keep focused on your dreams and do all you can to activate them. Beware of loss of energy or a sudden dullness in a relationship. Both may have a root cause you are ignoring. Look for the signs that will help you see more clearly where you are going and what you really want.

Gabriel asks:

What would your life look like with inspiration at its heart?

The Green Astronomer is represented by Nicolaus Copernicus (1473–1543), the first astronomer to effectively state that the sun did not revolve around the earth, but rather the earth revolved around the sun. Dee was certainly familiar with the work of Copernicus and made extensive use of his astronomical calculations, although Dee never openly supported the heliocentric theory, which was still regarded as heretical. Like Dee, Copernicus was a mathematician, astronomer, and physician, as well as a diplomat and economist. Within the context of the *Oracle*, Copernicus speaks to the hidden connections between events that can often go unnoticed.

Oracle of the North

(WORK/LIVING)

If your work affects others, be sure it is as pure and clear as you can make it. Remember that others may look up to you or rely on your strengths and abilities to further their own work. You are not alone in what you do. Even if you work or live in a competitive environment, remember that everything is interconnected in some way. Thus, your work is not only for you, and your life not lived for yourself alone.

Uriel asks:
How does your life or work affect others?

Oracle of the Centre

(GENERAL/PERSONAL)

Whatever unexpected turns that life has in store for you, there are always new ways to see the path ahead. You may think that you understand every aspect of your life, but there may be things that are less obvious and hidden from sight by circumstance or situation. Look for the hidden links between events, and you will find that your problems are less serious than you thought.

Oracle of the South

(INTENTION/DIRECTION)

When planning your future, always look at what your intentions really are. Don't think that because you have a great idea or the determination to proceed that the goal is necessarily a permanent thing. Always have a fallback position if you can. Changes at all kinds of unforeseeable levels can shift everything in a moment. Don't cling too hard to the past or the present if the future offers change.

Michael asks:
What has changed since you first thought of the idea?

Oracle of the East

(HEALTH/WELL-BEING)

Don't try to manage everything single-handedly, but accept the offers of help from others or, if necessary, ask for it. Those who make themselves into bastions of strength and determination can easily run out of energy and find themselves suffering from ill health or lack of motivation. Be aware of your limitations and pace yourself accordingly. Those who take things one step at a time are more likely to arrive at their destination.

Raphael asks:
When did you last ask for help? Who can support you now?

Gloriana's Blessing

My blessing to you is the ability to use your keen awareness of the patterns in life, some of which may indeed be reflected in the stars, and to advance your daily understanding of the influences that surround you.

Red Astronomer

JOHANNES KEPLER

Oracle of the West

(LOVE/INSPIRATION)

Love should never be seen as a negotiation, but rather as a shared experience. Take care of becoming the leading partner in your relationship and instead seek harmonious understandings that make friendship an essential part of every love story. When it comes to inspiration, practicality too has an important part to play. Although there will be times to seize the moment and be carried away on the tidal wave of ideas or passion, remember that the tide must withdraw at some point. Prepare for all eventualities.

Gabriel asks:

What remains when the tide of ideas or passion is withdrawn?

Johannes Kepler (1571–1630) represents the Red Astronomer. A contemporary of both Dee and Copernicus, he is credited with making improvements to the earliest refracting telescope, as well as setting forth the laws of planetary motion, upon which many succeeding astronomers based their work. Dee almost certainly met him at the court of Emperor Rudolf II of Austria (1552–1612). Like Dee, he was a profoundly religious man and argued for the standard version of the Creation at the time. Yet, he was also an astrologer and mathematician who was among the first to treat astronomy as a branch of physics. He understood how every aspect of life is related.

Oracle of the North

(WORK/LIVING)

Those with whom you work bring their own strengths to the table. Do not ignore them. The sharing of talents and skills is paramount in the creating of a good environment in which work and life can be nourished and grow strong. From the vitality of shared experiences come new and original things. Thus empowered, you will be able to extend your reach as far as you need.

Uriel asks:
What is the strength of a shared experience?

Oracle of the Centre

(GENERAL/PERSONAL)

As the worlds of others circulate around you, you will find your world touching theirs. When this happens, there is a magical exchange. You learn something from those with whom you come in contact; they learn from you. This relating of lives and energies, ideas, and feelings keeps the world in which we live filled with power and joy. If you find yourself in a difficult situation, seek this strength that will reempower you.

Oracle of the East

(HEALTH/WELL-BEING)

By being aware of the ways that energy underlies all things, you can learn to be strong. Whatever problems you face, remember that they can contribute to your reservoir of strength. Be mindful that life can present many unexpected challenges, but they have power over you only if you give in to them. Waste no opportunity to learn, even from the most-painful situations.

Raphael asks:
What can you learn from triumph or crisis?

Oracle of the South

(INTENTION/DIRECTION)

Whatever direction life takes you in, you will be faced with questions that require answers. Questions in themselves can help you evaluate your own ideas and those of others. Even the most-basic questionings prompt a response that can take you into new areas of intent. Always listen to such indicators and never feel that you can ask the same question too many times. Keep looking for bridges and signs that will guide you toward your intended goal.

Michael asks:
How do you question the questioners?

Gloriana's Blessing

My blessing to you is this: Learn to harbour your strengths and keep your focus close to best minister to the daily patterns of life. Do this while still enabling the joy of life.

Gold Astronomer

JOHN DEE

Oracle of the West

(LOVE/INSPIRATION)

It can be a good thing to look more deeply into the reasons for attraction, both in your partner and in the aspects of life that most inspire you. The bringing together of two beings, as with the marriage of elements in the alchemical process, can be both productive and challenging. Remember to look beyond the flash point of love or inspiration toward potential development and future.

Gabriel asks:
What path is paved by your love and service?

Dee himself takes on the role of the Gold Astronomer. His studies in astronomy were closely interwoven with his theories of navigation and mathematics. He believed it was possible to measure the "rays of celestial virtue" that emanated from the stars, thereby connecting astronomy to astrology in a completely new way. This work required thousands of precise calculations, filling many pages of Dee's notebooks. Within the *Oracle*, it means that he brings a cool and calculating eye to the measuring and solving of problems.

Oracle of the North

(WORK/LIVING)

As in alchemy, the elements that are gathered together produce something new. Be alert to new directions and objectives that both indicate a change of direction and point to new ways of perception. Seeing beyond the moment is immensely important, in life and work, and you should always look to both present and future to uncover your true destiny.

Uriel asks:
What new directions are being offered to you at this time?

Oracle of the Centre

(GENERAL/PERSONAL)

In the heat of the moment, you can be easily distracted from your intended goals. Excitement and the vitality of inspiration can lead you into places where you might not feel comfortable. It is important to understand not only what inspires you, but why. If everything you do brings challenges, ask if you are really following the right path.

Oracle of the East

(HEALTH/WELL-BEING)

Check the balance of your spiritual as well as physical health as often as you can. In the rush to achieve your goals, you may forget to give yourself time. Even if you have no specific spiritual viewpoint, remember that the essence of your being needs to be nourished just as much as your body. Feed your consciousness with music, literature, and art whenever you can. Wisdom is everywhere.

Raphael asks:
What works of art nourish and inspire you?

Oracle of the South

(INTENTION/DIRECTION)

Where do you see yourself five years from now? If your answer is "still in the same place," ask yourself: Why? Are you nourished by the sense of achievement that life is giving you, or could new directions be calling? This doesn't mean you should make changes for the sake of it, but rather that new directions and goals can revitalise you. Complacency can be your enemy.

Michael asks:
What guiding voice are you not listening to?

Gloriana's Blessing

My blessing to you is to remember the lessons of the past while looking forward to the blessings yet to come. Thus, I offer balance to the present time—when all shall be harmonious.

Silver Astronomer

GALILEO GALILEI

Oracle of the West

(LOVE/INSPIRATION)

Sometimes we sacrifice our independence to please another. This is something that should always be considered, since it can lead to resentment and doubt later. If you feel inspired to go in a new direction and your partner is not happy about this, give yourself time to discuss calmly and equitably every aspect of your course of action. You do not have to be selfish in order to proceed.

Gabriel asks:

What sacrifices does your life ask you to make?

The great Galileo Galilei (1564–1642) stands as the Silver Astronomer. His groundbreaking improvements to the early telescope and his discovery of the phases of Venus and the four largest moons of Jupiter make him a pivotal figure in the history of science. His advocacy of heliocentrism—the idea that the sun is the centre of the solar system—led to accusations of heresy, and he spent the last quarter of his life under house arrest, where he wrote several key books. In the *Oracle*, Galileo represents a deepening awareness of perception that enables the reader to see to the heart of an issue.

Oracle of the North

(WORK/LIVING)

Looking for the right path to follow can be just as challenging as staying on it. Consider the relationships that have brought you to where you are today. If you are about to embark on a new strategy, reflect on the impulse that led you to it. Examine the various links in the chain carefully. Is one weaker than the rest? How strong are you? Being prepared for any eventuality can save you a great deal of trouble.

Uriel asks:
What is your greatest strength?

Oracle of the Centre

(GENERAL/PERSONAL)

If you are a determined person but easily distracted, you may be tempted to make wrong decisions if the outcome appears attractive. Look deeper until you are certain of the most-likely effects of your choice. Review your life plan. You may feel unusually tired and lacking motivation, but if you allow yourself to look beyond surface appearances, you will discover new reserves of energy and fresh motivation.

Oracle of the South

(INTENTION/DIRECTION)

Allow yourself the freedom to choose what direction you will follow throughout your life. It is all too easy to get stuck in a rut, following a course that gives neither satisfaction nor reward. If this sounds familiar to you, take a step back, give your progress a long hard look, and consider what other options might be open to you. All kinds of influences push us toward making a choice, but every turn in the path should be carefully considered before taking it.

Michael asks:
What impels you to follow the path you are on?

Oracle of the East

(HEALTH/WELL-BEING)

If you are prone to weakness or attacks of ill health, you should look beyond the physical for the cause. While you should not neglect yourself or the advice of a qualified physician if the need arises, certain aspects of sickness can arise from a lack of self-esteem or from traumas buried in the history of your family. Be alert for these things and look out for the more oblique answers provided by the Oracle. These may seem unrelated, but a careful exploration often results in clearer understanding of the root cause.

Raphael asks:
What are the abiding resources of your family line?

Gloriana's Blessing

The blessing I offer is that you find stability to withstand the daily challenges life ushers in. Remember to look to those closest to you for support and acknowledge the welcome respite of kindness.

4

The Astrologers

• FUTURES •

Dee believed implicitly that astrology, astronomy, and mathematics were parallel sciences that could affect each other. Ever the great measurer, he spent long periods of time measuring the relative distances between the earth and various stars and planets, according to which their influence was greater or lesser. He also regarded astrology as a branch of astral magic, in which the magician manipulated the power of the various astral bodies. Thus, if he wished to draw upon the powers of the moon, he had to know which plants, stones, and metals came under its influence. With this knowledge, he could construct a talisman that invoked the moon's energy. This was simply a lesser example of the power exerted by all the planets, moons, and stars over everyone. As Dee himself wrote: "We, also, daily may perceive, that man's body, and all other elemental bodies, are altered, disposed, ordered, pleasured, and displeasured, by the influential working of the sun, moon, and other stars and planets." Invisible rays flooded the world, Dee believed, affecting everything they touched. Thus, the power of the heavenly bodies, according to their distance from the earth, could affect everyone to a greater or lesser degree. Those versed in the knowledge of such things, such as Dee himself, could read and interpret their meanings though measurement and study of the relationships of one star or planet to another.

Within the system of *The John Dee Oracle*, the astrologers, including Dee himself, are particularly relevant to future events. Therefore, if you are seeking the possible outcome of an issue you are currently dealing with, it is wise to pay close attention to the advice of the astrologers. However, it is important to remember that such readings suggest only one of several possible outcomes and should never be regarded as an unchangeable prediction. The clearer you focus on the question, the clearer the answer will be—but it remains just one answer among many.

Green Astrologer

ROBERT FLUDD

Oracle of the West

(LOVE/INSPIRATION)

In matters of the heart, we may feel helpless to direct our lives in the direction we know is most appropriate. Similarly, when inspiration strikes, we can get so caught up in the fire of the moment that we give way too easily. Consider the paths that lead to order and harmony, to a balanced state of being. Don't be too exclusive or try to shine without considering what others have to offer. Remember that you are part of a greater whole, and that the universe does not ignore you.

Gabriel asks:

If you follow a solitary path, what are the causes of this?

The Green Astrologer is represented by Robert Fludd (1574–1637), who was famous for his theories of celestial harmony and is remembered as a physician who followed the practices of Paracelsus. He was also a practising occultist and very possibly a member of the Rosicrucian Brotherhood, a mysterious group of esotericists who integrated many of the more magical philosophies of the time. Fludd likewise studied Qabalah and debated the merits of a mystical, rather than scientific, approach to knowledge with Kepler. Within the *Oracle*, he represents a mystical interpretation and solution to issues.

Oracle of the North

(WORK/LIVING)

Be aware of the magical element in your life. Magic is more than just incantations and spells. It is also intuition, inspiration, and a sense of wonder that permeates everything. What signs do you see around you that may have bearing on your issues? How often have your innate perceptions led you to make a decision that changed your life? Whatever problems you face now, try to sense the influence of deeper forces that can shift your perspective and even influence the way you relate to life.

Uriel asks:
What magic would you invite back into your life?

Oracle of the Centre

(GENERAL/PERSONAL)

Wherever you find yourself in life, you should remember that there is more than one way to perceive your journey. Ultimately, you may crave satisfaction and a sense of achievement, but there can be other ways to see this that are still personal but transcend the everyday. The influence of heavenly bodies is often overlooked or dismissed as superstition, but be assured that there are many forces in the universe we are not aware of. Such forces can and do affect our course through life and should not be ignored.

Oracle of the South

(INTENTION/DIRECTION)

Whenever you set out on a new path or reach a point where the ways divide, and you are uncertain which course of action to take, consider the deeper issues that may not be as clearly signposted as the surface meanings. If you are intuitive, test the strength of your instincts; if you are a pragmatist, remember that more-subtle forces may be at play. Reflect and weigh your options carefully before rushing into action.

Michael asks:
How does fate shape your life?

Oracle of the East

(HEALTH/WELL-BEING)

Whatever issues you face, try to approach them holistically, considering not just the outer signs but delving deeper into the underlying causes. If you are unwell or unhappy, there may be more than one reason. Do not overlook the physical signs, since they can lead to healing or fresh insight, but also consider what else might be influencing you. Above all, do not give up. Be aware that other avenues exist, and strive to find and follow them, wherever they may lead. Remember that help is always available if you truly seek it.

Raphael asks:
What fuels hopelessness and what is the alternative?

Gloriana's Blessing

My blessing to you is one of harmony and restoration. When life seems to be breaking apart, seek the song of the spheres and attune yourself to their notes of hope and joy.

Red Astrologer

WILLIAM LILLY

Oracle of the West

(LOVE/INSPIRATION)

No matter where you find love or inspiration, both require regular maintenance and care. Neglecting a relationship can cause it to fail; neglecting inspiration may cause it to wither and die. Taking time out of a busy life to nurture your relationships—both personal and work related—will keep them fresh and alive. Such things are easily overlooked in the rush to achieve material success. Be mindful to honour every aspect of your relationships, including those with the wider world, as often as you can.

Gabriel asks:

What part of your life are you neglecting?

William Lilly (1602–81) stands in the role of the Red Astrologer. Lilly was one of the most renowned astrologers of his time, particularly famed for the accuracy of the charts he created to predict future events. In 1652, he is said to have predicted the Great Fire of London, some fourteen years before it occurred. Some even accused him of starting the fire, and he was tried for the offence but found innocent. His greatest work, *Christian Astrology*, published in 1647, is still regarded as one of the most important texts on traditional astrology. Beginning in 1648, Lilly issued a series of astrological almanacs in which he successfully predicted national events during the English Civil War. His presence in the *Oracle* is his ability to read the signs of future events.

Oracle of the North

(WORK/LIVING)

Ideally, life should be a unified whole in which every aspect—work, love, knowledge, and truth—comes together to form a path you can follow. Such a structure requires constant attention, and neglecting one of the many strands that make up your life may throw the rest out of balance. Consider every aspect of your being as part of a greater whole, and remember that life truly is a "life's work," requiring ongoing maintenance and care.

Uriel asks:
Do the many parts of your life constitute a whole?

Oracle of the Centre

(GENERAL/PERSONAL)

Many strands intertwine to form a single path, and we often overlook the hidden influences beneath the surface of events. Similarly, it's easy to underestimate the impact of others who come into your sphere of influence or whose qualities affect the way you make decisions. Imagine yourself for a moment as a hub around which many stars constellate. Are you the only one who matters here? Or do the qualities and abilities of others play a role in everything you envision?

Oracle of the East

(HEALTH/WELL-BEING)

You need to give attention to every aspect of your life, including health and well-being. To neglect any one aspect can lead to a general detriment, and you may find yourself getting drawn more and more deeply into a position from which it is increasingly hard to recover. If there are things in your life that you have neglected, now is the time to give them your attention and to be open to the repercussions of ignoring significant signs.

Raphael asks:
Why neglect signs that show you the way?

Oracle of the South

(INTENTION/DIRECTION)

Sometimes, even the most outwardly successful and profitable aspects of your journey may need attention. Do not allow yourself to become complacent or neglect the care required to nurture your dreams. Remember the constellations of strength and inspiration that surround you at all times, even in the darkest moments. Draw strength from the friends and helpers, both physical and spiritual, who support you.

Michael asks:
To what pathway is your dream life directing you?

Gloriana's Blessing

My blessing is one of calmness and certainty. Though your way may seem doubtful, I assure you that if you look to the wisdom of the stars, you shall find rest and recovery.

Gold Astrologer

SIMON FORMAN

Oracle of the West

(LOVE/INSPIRATION)

The search for inspiration and happiness are indissolubly linked. When you set out on a new course of action, be careful to remember the ways that these things are related and how they impinge on your inner as well as outer life. It is all too easy to neglect aspects of your life that can teach you things you need to be aware of. Spread your consciousness as wide as you can, and be sensitive to the connections between one point and another.

Gabriel asks:

What is the furthest point of your inspiration or attraction?

Perhaps one of the most famous astrologers of all time, Simon Forman (1552–1611) stands in the role of Gold Astrologer. Forman spent the first half of his life studying ancient texts and then-modern treatises before immersing himself in the hidden life of London. From 1583, he set up as a physician, basing his diagnoses and treatments on spiritual knowledge. He kept detailed records of his patients, documenting everything from their illnesses to their marriage prospects. Forman is said to have predicted his own death with chilling accuracy. His intuitive approach to astrology makes him a valuable ally in the interpretation of signs.

Oracle of the North
(WORK/LIVING)

Do not try to stand alone, but, rather, share your burdens with others who are willing to do so. The work of several people is often more powerful and substantial than that of one. Even though you may see yourself as a leader who commands those around you, remember that a community that lives and works in harmony can achieve far more than a single person struggling to hold everything together.

Uriel asks:
How will you inspire others to work with you?

Oracle of the Centre
(GENERAL/PERSONAL)

Wherever your path leads, be alert to the signposts indicating where the road divides. This is important because it is all too easy to miss a vital turning that could lead to a new direction, one that may offer better prospects than the course you have been following. Paying attention to these diverging streams can help you become more successful and recognised as a leader and guide.

Oracle of the East
(HEALTH/WELL-BEING)

Consider how everything that surrounds you—whether individuals or groups, places or possessions—is part of a whole. Remember, too, that your health and well-being are not separate from the circumstances around you but are part of a greater pattern, one you may or may not be aware of. Seek out hidden resonances with people and places that make you feel more complete.

Raphael asks:
What brings you the deepest sense of connection?

Oracle of the South
(INTENTION/DIRECTION)

How you orient yourself in your daily life is of the utmost importance. Though you may feel yourself drawn to the light of the sun, remember that too long an exposure to its rays can burn you. Consider the other directions and the elements they embody, and see what they have to offer. Will the waters hold you up, will the air help you to breathe better, will the earth support you?

Michael asks:
What power or direction draws you the most?

Gloriana's Blessing

My blessing is this: that you find the path you seek and recognise it when you reach it, and that your journey is clear and full of wonder. Be sure your goal is near.

Silver Astrologer

JOHN DEE

Oracle of the West

(LOVE/INSPIRATION)

The best relationships are those founded not only on love but also on understanding. A true partnership draws equally on the strengths of both partners. Stresses and strains in any relationship are easily created but less easily resolved. Begin as you mean to continue, by finding points of agreement and recognising areas that are more sensitive than others. Allow yourself to be inspired by the complexities of the world, rather than by any single aspect.

Gabriel asks:

What are your strongest areas of agreement or disagreement?

Dee himself appears in the role of the Silver Astrologer. Astrology was immensely important to Dee and permeated every aspect of his life. His horoscopes for Queen Mary and the future Queen Elizabeth first brought him to the attention of the English court, and wherever he travelled, he was invited to prepare charts for the highest-ranking nobles in the land. The ebb and flow of celestial tides remained a subject of study for him throughout the rest of his life. In the *Oracle*, he functions as an interpreter of the many tides that still influence us, whether of the planets or the everyday concerns of daily life.

Oracle of the North

(WORK/LIVING)

Remember that you are not alone in your journey through life. Though you may answer to only yourself, both in work and daily life, you should still be aware of the lives that cross and interact with your own. Creativity also comes from many sources and is rarely the product of a single mind or spirit. The weaving of creation includes your dreams and hopes as well as countless others. Draw upon this resource in all that you do.

Uriel asks:

What do your dreams and waking visions show you?

Oracle of the Centre

(GENERAL/PERSONAL)

Many levels of connection between this world and the others exist. Some come through the influence of the stars and planets, others through the realms of nature, spirit, and matter. None should be excluded in your search for truth, meaning, and fulfilment. Understand that you are part of the great weaving of the cosmos, in which humanity is neither more nor less important than the plants, the animals, or the elements around you.

Oracle of the South

(INTENTION/DIRECTION)

Accepting your limitations gives you greater strength to focus on the issue at hand while also helping you attune to the direction you need to take next. If you are prone to overextending yourself, consider the elements in your life that either cause stress or create a more comfortable state of being. No matter how high your ambition, remember that without a strong and balanced foundation, you may crash and burn.

Michael asks:

What is the next step you need to take?

Oracle of the East

(HEALTH/WELL-BEING)

Living at full stretch all the time can be just as challenging as adopting a more relaxed approach to life. A wiser person will strive to balance these two extremes, neither overextending themselves emotionally or physically, nor becoming too complacent and static. To some, the middle way may seem dull or safe, but discovering the perfect point of balance both is invigorating and promotes happiness and a healthy life.

Raphael asks:

Where is the point of balance in your life?

Gloriana's Blessing

My blessing to you is that the tides of life do not sweep you before them, but that you are able to ride them out with grace and joyfulness. In the darkest moments, remember there are new mornings ahead.

5

The Geographers

• JOURNEYS •

Dee's interest in geography—both magical and physical—and in the relationship between landmasses began early in his life, when he encountered the great mapmaker Mercator. Dee returned from a sojourn in Belgium with one of the first globes to accurately represent the world. Later, he used his skills as a geographer and historian to support elaborate claims for Elizabeth I over regions such as Greenland, Ireland, and the North Polar region. His 1578 work, *The Limits of the British Empire* (a term he coined), was highly influential. Dee's extensive knowledge of navigation is evident in his significant book *General and Rare Memorials Pertaining to the Perfect Art of Navigation*. Originally in four volumes—though only one survives—its publication in 1577 made Dee an indispensable consultant for planning major voyages. He is known to have advised explorers such as Drake, Cabot, and Humphrey Gilbert. As a reward for his guidance on planning a route to the New World, Gilbert granted Dee the rights to all lands discovered north of the fifty-ninth parallel, which, had the voyage succeeded, would have meant that Dee owned most of Canada. However, the voyage failed.

It is even speculated that Dee, an inveterate traveler in search of wisdom, planned to sail to Asia, though this never happened. Even in the single surviving volume, we see the breadth and depth of his reading. For every city or sea route, he first gathered information from ancient sources, meticulously sifting through them for meaning and then corroborating his findings with the latest geographical and navigational writings. Dee's expertise as a map interpreter and his pursuit of the best routes between places make this aspect of his multifaceted character a perfect key for exploring matters related to an individual's life journey. In the context of the *Oracle*, the presence of any one of the geographers can point toward new directions or influences in an individual journey as well as showing a map of current situations.

Green Geographer

GERARDUS MERCATOR

Oracle of the West

(LOVE/INSPIRATION)

Love strikes us unexpectedly and without warning, often leaving us adrift on a sea of emotions. Keep in mind that the experiences of past relationships can help orient you in this new adventure. At times, you may feel uncertain about the best way to proceed, and in such moments, signs are invaluable. Look for the way through the rainbow mists with as much certainty and confidence as you can gather.

Gabriel asks:
What does this relationship say to your inner self?

Gerardus Mercator (1512–94) is the Green Geographer. A personal friend of Dee's, he is still renowned today as one of the first to construct a terrestrial globe accurate to within a few degrees. Mercator began as a maker of mathematical instruments but soon transitioned to mapmaking, producing some of the finest maps of the known world. Dee met him in Louvain, and the two men exchanged information for many years afterward. Dee brought one of the first Mercator globes back to England and used it, along with other data, in his quest to substantiate Queen Elizabeth's claim over various northern lands. In the *Oracle*, Mercator's work guides our own adventures.

Oracle of the North

(WORK/LIVING)

Wherever you find yourself located on your journey, remember to look around you and notice the key points that will help guide you to your required destination. Be careful not to rush ahead without orienting yourself first; otherwise you may find yourself lost. Whatever task you undertake, and whatever change in circumstance may occur, planning and observation will help you be prepared for whatever comes.

Uriel asks:

What signposts can you see around you?

Oracle of the Centre

(GENERAL/PERSONAL)

In the great adventure of life, you require signposts to help you find your way. Whenever you feel lost or abandoned, tune into the surroundings in which you find yourself. Remember that these are not necessarily the physical settings for your current position, but also the spiritual and circumstantial indicators of your journey. Consider yourself an explorer, seeking the way forward through territory that may sometimes be uncharted or may become a cause of anxiety when the ground seems uncertain beneath your feet.

Oracle of the East

(HEALTH/WELL-BEING)

Circumstances can change overnight, and you may find yourself uncertain of what direction or action to take next. Try to be prepared for all eventualities by looking ahead and by being aware of your inner health. The quality of life can be affected by many things, but if you remain alert, you will be able to overcome most obstacles in your path.

Raphael asks:

How do you stay in tune with yourself?

Oracle of the South

(INTENTION/DIRECTION)

It is very easy to lose your way amid the countless twists and turns of the path through life. While it may be difficult to look ahead far enough to plan a future direction, getting to a point from which you can see some way ahead is very helpful. When life gets complicated, try drawing a simple map on which the most-important aspects of the journey are marked. Even if you do no more than this, you will find your circumstances more understandable and be able to plan your next steps.

Michael asks:

What guidance do your look for on your journey?

Gloriana's Blessing

My blessing is for how you handle the things that trouble you. May you find a peaceful solution, one that leaves no wreckage in its wake, and one that is both fulfilling and glorious.

Red Geographer

MARCO POLO

Oracle of the West

(LOVE/INSPIRATION)

Inspiration can guide your steps along the road and may show you the way ahead in clearer outline than your ordinary everyday sense of sight. Be sensitive to the signals that come back to you from the signposts on the road ahead, and do not be afraid to take chances. Sometimes we get only one chance at a target.

Gabriel asks:

How clear is your sense of direction and intention?

Marco Polo (1254–1324) represents the Red Geographer. Born in Venice to a family of maritime traders, he embarked on an epic journey to the East in 1269, along with his father and brother, which lasted twenty-four years. His extraordinary voyage not only opened up trade routes but also increased awareness of the culture of the Mongolian Empire. During his travels, Marco visited Emperor Kublai Khan and briefly served as a courtier. He returned to Venice in 1293, only to find the city at war with Genoa, leading to his imprisonment. While in prison, he dictated the story of his voyage to a fellow prisoner. In the context of the *Oracle*, he stands for the courage needed to explore more deeply into territories where we would often prefer not to go.

Oracle of the North

(WORK/LIVING)

Though you may seek a spiritual answer to your problems, it is just as well to remember the physical and emotional aspect of things also. Your work may be subject to unforeseen change, or your life takes a new and unexpected direction, but if you are sufficiently connected to the real world, you will find it much easier to negotiate your current circumstances.

Uriel asks:
How do you strengthen your connection to the world around you?

Oracle of the Centre

(GENERAL/PERSONAL)

If the way ahead seems perilous, prepare yourself by considering the best options available to you. Have courage, because the signs are good and you have a good chance of coming out a winner. However, be wary of taking advice from anyone you do not know well, since they may seem well informed but do not necessarily know you well enough to offer reliable advice. Remember to look to every direction before you take any decision you may not be ready to take.

Oracle of the South

(INTENTION/DIRECTION)

Preparation and planning ahead are important, but do not allow yourself to be too caught up in the minutiae of life. Allow your sense of direction to unfold gradually, and enjoy the process. Hold the map you have projected in your mind but be willing to diverge from this path if new possibilities appear on the horizon. Remember, you are the captain of your own ship.

Michael asks:
What happens when you flow with the tides of life?

Oracle of the East

(HEALTH/WELL-BEING)

Being prepared for any unforeseen circumstance may seem overly proscriptive, but it is always wise. Though we may feel ourselves to be indestructible, we should be aware of our limitations and not try to exceed them. Map out the stages of your progression though life as far as possible without trying to force a direction that may be inappropriate or risky. Seek a balance between being overly organised and too unaware of where the road may lead.

Raphael asks:
How have unexpected changes altered your life's course?

Gloriana's Blessing

My blessing is that your voyage is clearly defined, and that you are not driven off course but are guided by those who care for you until you reach a safe harbour.

Gold Geographer

JOHN DEE

Oracle of the West

(LOVE/INSPIRATION)

If you have recently left behind a difficult relationship, now may be the time to look ahead to fresh possibilities. Do not cling too heavily to the past, but, rather, make yourself available to new opportunities. Whether you seek love or inspiration, the same is true—old and outworn truths may need to be discarded in order to make way for new ones, and a change of direction can restore your belief in yourself or others.

Gabriel asks:
What ideas or beliefs may be ready for replacement?

Dee himself stands as the Gold Geographer. Though it may be said that his interest lay as much in spiritual geography as in physical, his knowledge of maps and mapmaking was substantial. He advised on the first English attempt to find a route to Cathay (China), and several of the greatest sailors and adventurers of the time sought his guidance and assistance in creating maps. In this role, Dee helps us navigate the shoals of tough decisions and difficult issues, steering us with words of wisdom toward calmer waters.

Oracle of the North

(WORK/LIVING)

Be careful not to become so absorbed in the processes of living that you miss out on the joy of the experience itself. Do not tie yourself down to any single set of considerations; instead, keep a window open for new directions or opportunities to appear. Befriend the journey for its own sake, and be ready to follow your instincts when called upon.

Uriel asks:
What are your instincts telling you right now?

Oracle of the Centre

(GENERAL/PERSONAL)

Sometimes life can be dramatic, and our reaction to such events varies according to out nature. Always look for the true meaning behind the outward appearance, and seek to navigate around the shoals of disquiet and doubt that can beset us when we least expect them. Remember that others may be affected by these events, and try to keep everything in proportion. Be careful not to be inconsiderate or unfeeling.

Oracle of the East

(HEALTH/WELL-BEING)

If opportunities are offered to you that being new dimensions to your life—take them. A change of pace or a new location can bring release and healing. Take a look at the map of your life and see where you might like to go on holiday. Explore the inner landscape of your heart and soul. Look at every aspect of living for joy and wisdom—especially the less frequented ones.

Raphael asks:
Where do you look for the greatest happiness and healing?

Oracle of the South

(INTENTION/DIRECTION)

Sometimes it is necessary to explore the darker corners of your life to better understand how to find new direction and purpose. Always strive to be honest with yourself and those around you, and do not shy away from responsibility. Remember, when dark times arise, they cannot last forever—beyond them lie fresh waters and calmer seas.

Michael asks:
How are you best able to face your deepest fears?

Gloriana's Blessing

My blessing is that you may look with clear sight at the path ahead, see where the road leads, understand its harsher places, and respond to life's challenges with grace and equanimity.

Silver Geographer

FRANCIS DRAKE

Oracle of the West

(LOVE/INSPIRATION)

The best way to explore the landscape of a relationship is to listen to the other person's view and learn the deeper side of their nature. Don't try to dominate, any more than you should give in to every request. Instead, look at the many facets of your beloved's character, which are seldom as straightforward as you may think. Your ability to listen and respond is all important and should be cultivated as much as possible.

Gabriel asks:

How carefully are you listening?

Francis Drake (1540–96) remains one of the most well-known and inspiring figures of the Elizabethan era. A skilled sailor and navigator, he was also a privateer who seized immense wealth from Spanish treasure ships, and as a soldier, he served as second in command of the English fleet against the Spanish Armada. His greatest achievement, however, was his circumnavigation of the globe between 1577 and 1580. Dee would almost certainly have known him. Drake was so despised by the Spanish that they placed a reward of 20,000 ducats (around £4 million / $6.5 million) on his head. In the *Oracle*, he represents the ability to forge ahead in any situation, no matter how great the opposition may be.

Oracle of the North

(WORK/LIVING)

Before setting forth on a new journey, you should take a careful reading of any signs that are apparent. If these suggest that you should not undertake the journey, do not do so. Remember that each new day is a new opportunity to change direction, to find new approaches to your work and life, and to acknowledge truths that you have always known but not necessarily seen for what they can tell you.

Uriel asks:
What changes are offered to you now?

Oracle of the Centre

(GENERAL/PERSONAL)

As you navigate the shoals of daily life, try to put down roots or set markers so that, if needed, you can return to these earlier places and explore them again. Old and neglected paths may sometimes offer more than you realise, and it's best not to assume that you're done with something until you have mapped every aspect of its landscape. Remember, too, that for every outer aspect, there is an inner one, and even if you're not inclined toward spiritual exploration, you should still be aware of every part of a situation.

Oracle of the South

(INTENTION/DIRECTION)

Whatever your intention or direction in life, it rarely happens in isolation. Be open to the advice and inspiration that others may offer. Going it alone can be exciting, and if it's necessary, you will find the reserves of energy you need. However, in most cases, you should be able to lean on others, conserving your strength for the burst of speed required to carry you across the finish line.

Michael asks:
Are you able to trust those who offer you help?

Oracle of the East

(HEALTH/WELL-BEING)

There are times when strength may fail you, when even to put one foot in front of the other may become difficult. This can be a health issue, or something deeper. It can be the cause of depression or simply lethargy. You should fight against this with every fibre of your being. Do not confuse this experience with simple exhaustion or the need for a rest. Keep awake to the options offered to you, seek progress by easy stages, but never let your chances slip away though lack of concentration and energy.

Raphael asks:
Why are you feeling exhausted?

Gloriana's Blessing

I offer you the blessing of honesty, the ability to see beyond the surface of your issues, and the strength to ride out the harshest periods of your life until you emerge into fresh morning light.

6

The Physicians

• WELL-BEING •

Today, we are accustomed to thinking of physicians as white-coated doctors in hospitals or general practitioners at local health centres. However, the origins of medicine stretch far into the past, and while early physicians knew little about the physical body and internal organs, they possessed intuitive skills that far surpassed many working in medicine today. In Dee's time, diagnoses were often made using astrology, and the medicines of the day owed more to alchemy than to chemistry. Dee himself was awarded a doctorate in medicine from the University of Cracow (Poland) in 1583, although he never seems to have practised. He did, however, write extensively about the preparation of alchemical tinctures with healing properties and, during his service to Queen Elizabeth I, claimed several times that he could produce the Philosopher's Stone, known to possess healing powers.

Dee maintained a lifelong fascination with the workings of the human body and its connection to the spirit. His personal library reflected this, containing numerous early works on anatomy and proto-medicine. As with all of Dee's studies, medicine was deeply integrated into his belief that everything was connected, and that no discipline was without its magical aspect. Within the context of *The John Dee Oracle*, health and well-being are not merely physical but also spiritual. As many alternative practitioners will attest, physical ailments often stem from spiritual imbalance. The advice offered by the four physicians—represented here by some of the great early practitioners of the healing arts—should therefore be understood in this light.

Green Physician

PARACELSUS

Oracle of the West

(LOVE/INSPIRATION)

It is just as important to keep your relationships and emotions healthy as it is to care for your body. When life runs smoothly and inspiration flows easily, you are in a state of balance. However, if things feel awkward or blocked, whether in love or inspiration, you should take time to explore the reasons behind this. Most problems can be resolved with effort and attention.

Gabriel asks:
What brings you together or splits you apart?

The Green Physician is represented by Paracelsus (1493–1541), a German Swiss doctor who shared many of Dee's interests—including alchemy, astrology, and esotericism. Paracelsus displayed an early aptitude for medicine. His wanderings took him throughout Europe, Asia Minor, and even in Africa, always in pursuit of hidden knowledge. Astrology was a very important part of Paracelsus's approach to medicine, and he devoted space in all his writings to the construction of astrological talismans for curing disease. Within the *Oracle*, he offers a deeper level of diagnosis across the varied aspects of life.

Oracle of the North

(WORK/LIVING)

If work is becoming too much for you, try to stay in a relaxed frame of mind and make time to take regular breaks. Even five minutes sitting in a chair and breathing evenly, or taking a brisk walk around the block, can restore flagging energies and will more than repay the time taken.

Uriel asks:
What arises in stillness?

Oracle of the East

(HEALTH/WELL-BEING)

Everyone is prone to losing balance from time to time, which can result in sickness or depression. Identify areas in your life where you feel less balanced or overwhelmed, and do not hesitate to seek advice. Exercise caution before undertaking activities that might overwhelm your body. Be mindful of your limitations before accepting a challenge that could have a negative impact on your health.

Rafael asks:
When challenging prospects are ahead, what resources aid you?

Oracle of the Centre

(GENERAL/PERSONAL)

Healing should be accepted wholeheartedly and without question. Belief in the doctor or the healing art is a vital part of recovery. In the rhythms of daily life, we experience both great heights and great depths, and there will be times when your physical body lacks the energy to meet such challenges. As with all things, balance is crucial; look to every aspect of your life to find the spaces where you can rest and recuperate. Health and well-being cross all boundaries of life and are not solely about physical states.

Oracle of the South

(INTENTION/DIRECTION)

Be sure to make the best possible use of your native wisdom to keep your life on the right track. If you feel yourself slipping out of your regular pattern of being, check to make sure that whichever direction you are being led in is one that you wish for and not something forced upon you.

Michael asks:
What is the right path for you?

Gloriana's Blessing

My blessing to you is that you are aware of the truth underlying all that occurs, that you do not lose your way in the many turning points of your life, and that you find healing whenever it is required.

Red Physician

GALEN OF PERGAMON

Oracle of the West

(LOVE/INSPIRATION)

If love is your guiding star, follow it to the source, but be cautious of becoming sidetracked and losing your way in the emotional turmoil of relationships. Few people are so well matched that they agree on everything, but a resolution should eventually be sought, even in the stormiest of alliances. The journey from love to inspiration is filled with ageless wonder, but if you are easily swayed, be mindful of accepting everything offered in the name of love.

Gabriel asks:

What do you truly seek in another?

The Red Physician is represented by Galen of Pergamon (129–200 CE), possibly the most accomplished medical practitioner of the ancient world. Galen made significant contributions to a variety of scientific disciplines, including anatomy, physiology, pathology, pharmacology, and neurology. He travelled extensively, gathering medical knowledge and theories before settling in Rome, where he became the personal physician to several emperors. Galen's theories influenced Western medical science for nearly two millennia, and his studies of anatomy remained largely uncontested until the sixteenth century. Medical students continued to study his writings well into the nineteenth century. Dee himself would have been familiar with Galen's work. His presence in the *Oracle* proffers good medical advice.

Oracle of the North

(WORK/LIVING)

There may be areas in your life that you are neglecting—especially if you work too hard and do not give yourself enough time to restore your natural energy levels. Be especially wary of old problems that have been put aside to be dealt with later and then left to fester and grow strong. Look for the deeper causes of stresses and moodiness, since these are seldom as obvious as they seem.

Uriel asks:
What are the true causes of disquiet?

Oracle of the Centre

(GENERAL/PERSONAL)

Good health is about maintaining balance at every level of your life. Not only should you pay attention to your diet, take regular exercise, and get sufficient sleep, but you should also care for your inner health—the spiritual vitality that comes from living in harmony with the universe. This balance doesn't happen automatically; it requires effort and energy. If you are feeling weak or out of alignment, spend some time each day restoring the natural balance you should feel toward everything and everyone in your life.

Oracle of the South

(INTENTION/DIRECTION)

Whatever your goals, it is important to maintain a balance between appearance and content. Showy productions are often hollow and without substance. Always keep in mind the first moment of inspiration that set you on a particular course, and stay as true as you can to that spark. If you feel drawn toward a huge deviation from your normal path, consider this carefully and check your inner compass.

Michael asks:
Where is this path really leading you?

Oracle of the East

(HEALTH/WELL-BEING)

If you are experiencing bouts of ill health or feeling constantly exhausted, look for the deeper causes of these. Do not ignore signs of illness (early treatment is more likely to resolve such things), but do not be satisfied with the simple levels of preventive medicine. Many forms of sickness are caused by older, unresolved issues that will take hold only more powerfully if you ignore them over a long period of time.

Raphael asks:
Are you aware of imbalances in your life?

Gloriana's Blessing

My blessing to you is that you understand the meaning of true health, and that when you are sick and fearful, you remain aware of the inner strength that keeps you on the path you wish to follow. May health surround you always.

Gold Physician

HIPPOCRATES OF KOS

Oracle of the West

(LOVE/INSPIRATION)

Whatever the moment you are in tells you, look beyond it to observe the bigger picture. If you feel doubtful or crestfallen, remember the times you felt strong and positive. Whenever a good moment comes, explore every aspect of it until you know it thoroughly, so that you can recall it at times of fear or when your resolution fails you.

Gabriel asks:

When was the last high point in your life?

The Gold Physician is represented by the early Greek doctor and philosopher Hippocrates of Kos (460–ca. 550 BCE). Imprisoned for twenty years due to his teachings about the human body, he wrote several medical works during his incarceration, many of which contain ideas still widely accepted today. Hippocrates was likely trained at the temple of Asclepios, the god of medicine, in Kos. Throughout his life, he taught and practised medicine, travelling across the ancient world. He died in Larissa, aged between eighty-three and ninety, though some accounts suggest he lived to be over one hundred.

Oracle of the North

(WORK/LIVING)

Learn to be satisfied by the measure of success and financial reward you receive from your work. Focus on the level of satisfaction that everything you do gives back to you, the things that inspire you to continue growing and developing. Don't mix work with pleasure more than you need to, but don't compartmentalise the areas of your life either. Allow delight in what you do to communicate itself to other people, and share the wisdom you acquire along the way.

Uriel asks:
How much do life and work contribute to your personal growth?

Oracle of the Centre

(GENERAL/PERSONAL)

How did you come to this point in your life? Who or what helped you and who or what blocked your progress? If you can follow the strand of your life to this moment, you will be stronger and more assured. Even if you do not believe that anything is preordained, you may yet become aware of links and parallels between crucial points in your journey. Recognising these can give you insight into the next steps to take and affect your general state of health and well-being.

Oracle of the East

(HEALTH/WELL-BEING)

Spread your net as far as possible in every aspect of life. Look for new and original ways to make your mark. Embrace all that you do and try to share the wonder of life and creativity. Balancing every aspect of your daily life—the good and the bad—allows you to know what you are doing and why you are who you are. Listen to good advice and consider all your options before deciding.

Raphael asks:
Who or what fills you with the greatest delight?

Oracle of the South

(INTENTION/DIRECTION)

When you know where you want to go in life, give it everything you have. It is easy to forget who you are and why you started a particular venture or relationship, both in business and personally. When you are in full flight, follow your heart, but remember to pause and take stock whenever you can. Stay true to your vision, and do not let the negative responses of others, or your own inner doubts, hinder your progress.

Michael asks:
Are you a leader or a follower?

Gloriana's Blessing

My blessing is that you find your way through the shoals of life with the minimum of challenges. But do not forget that sometimes the things that offer opposition also offer growth and renewed strength.

Silver Physician

JOHN DEE

Oracle of the West

(LOVE/INSPIRATION)

Be as honest as you can with yourself, whether in matters of the heart or the head. Self-delusion is common and is difficult to recognise or reverse. Whenever you feel caught up in a powerful stream of life, look for the signs of unrealistic options that may never transpire, and do not let yourself be distracted by elation. Remember that even the most inspirational person or idea can still have its negative side.

Gabriel asks:

What aspect of a situation is most important to you?

The Silver Physician is represented by Dee himself in this aspect of his multifaceted life. As noted above, he was awarded a doctorate in medicine at the University of Cracow (Poland) in 1583. However, there is no evidence that he ever actually practiced, though he did write at length about the preparation of alchemical tinctures with healing properties. Dee seems to have discovered an almost homeopathic method of healing, which involved multiplying the medicinal properties of a mysterious red powder by multiples of ten until it reached a degree of potency that could heal every known ailment. In the context of the *Oracle*, Dee's knowledge of medicine makes him an important repository for spiritual healing.

Oracle of the North

(WORK/LIVING)

What truths do you bring to the furtherance of your work and life? No matter how strong your convictions may be that you are right, you should always be aware that others are possessed of just as strong ideas and that to ignore them or try to overset them is not a wise thing to do. Whether you are just setting forth on your life journey or have lived out most of your years, treat every moment as the opportunity for a new beginning.

Uriel asks:
Where does wisdom reside for you?

Oracle of the Centre

(GENERAL/PERSONAL)

In all things, you should try to find a vantage point, physical or spiritual, from which you can see all that you are doing and where your current direction is taking you. Look to the mystery of the stars and the significance of dates that are special to you. Above all, be courageous and do not give in to fear or sadness, no matter what the odds. Respect yourself and be as honest as you can in everything you do. These are the principles of a good life.

Oracle of the South

(INTENTION/DIRECTION)

Whatever point in your life you have reached, whatever season most empowers you, remember to be as rooted as you can in the rich soil of your own innate wisdom. No matter from what quarter the wind blows, or where they would seem to send you, remain true to your own inner compass and follow the dictates of your heart. Take time to consider the path you are on and all that it may bring you.

Michael asks:
What guides you most—logic or intuition?

Oracle of the East

(HEALTH/WELL-BEING)

Seek the truth that is everywhere around you. Use the power of your imagination, and your inner spiritual certainty, to guide your steps. Consider the envelope of the body as a sacred vessel, which you will maintain truthfully and honourably. Look for the positive aspects of every situation before allowing the negative to enter. If you are feeling sorrowful, angry, or despairing, take time to address the causes of these moods before you move forward.

Raphael asks:
What do you need to maintain your physical strength and health?

Gloriana's Blessing

My blessing is that you have access to patience when the frustrations of the journey are too great. Sickness may be a burden, but it can also teach us more than we realise.

7

The Historians

• MAP OF LIFE •

Dee's approach to history was not that of the more usual study of peoples, places, and the tides of time. Rather, he took an intuitive and mystical approach, looking specifically for patterns of esoteric meaning, ancient beliefs that he could reconcile with his Christian faith. This led him into some unusual areas, including the stories of King Arthur. At this time there was no knowledge of the possible historicity of this character, though he was still regarded as a real king. Dee used the traditions surrounding King Arthur to assert Queen Elizabeth I's right to various lands—stretching as far north as the polar region, where Dee claimed that Arthur had once ruled over a great city. In the context of the *Oracle*, Dee's historical studies reflect questions of life direction and personal history. Anyone seeking to explore the inner patterns of their life (coincidences for which there is no easy explanation) would do well to pay attention to the presence of any of the five historians in a reading.

Green Historian

HERODOTUS

Oracle of the West

(LOVE/INSPIRATION)

Often, we spend much of our time waiting for significant events to occur, such as finding the right life partner and setting up a home. However, remember that other things can motivate us just as powerfully as love, and not everyone is suited to share their lives at the deepest level. If you feel inclined to live a solitary life, embrace it and enjoy it fully.

Gabriel asks:

Do you prefer to live alone or with others?

Herodotus (ca. 484–425 BCE) represents the Green Historian. Often called the "Father of History," he was the first to systematically collect materials, test their accuracy where possible, and arrange them into a well-constructed and vivid narrative. *The Histories*, his only surviving work, was certainly known to Dee, who would have admired Herodotus's careful approach to his sources and his curiosity about everything. His appearance in the Oracle signals a deepening sense of how things fit together.

Oracle of the North

(WORK/LIVING)

If you find yourself looking for ways to build bridges between one idea or situation and another, look for tried-and-tested means of working. Just because an event took place in the past does not mean it is redundant. And remember that if you cannot see the wood for the trees, this does not mean there is no solution. Try relating the events as a story to yourself—watch out for points of influence and overlap.

Uriel asks:
How does the current situation reflect older experiences?

Oracle of the Centre

(GENERAL/PERSONAL)

What patterns can you observe in your daily life? Almost anything that takes place can have a bearing on your own journey, and remembering past events can point to new ways of understanding current issues. Never ignore signs from previous situations, and do all you can to find connections between events. Remember that you can draw upon the experience of others, past and present, to help point to the best way to deal with an issue happening at this moment. History remains one of our best and most-overlooked teachers.

Oracle of the South

(INTENTION/DIRECTION)

Consider what really makes you happy. Many people think they know and understand what happiness is, only to find that when viewed closely, it melts away. A great many people believe that the only objective in their life is to be happy, ignoring the truth that shows them that there are other things that can bring contentment and provide a significant focus. Whatever direction life takes you, consider the many and varied reasons for doing all that you do.

Michael asks:
How do you define happiness?

Oracle of the East

(HEALTH/WELL-BEING)

Connections exist everywhere in your life. Look for patterns as you follow the path ahead. In matters of health, too, you will find mirrors that connect cause and effect. Look beyond the surface of events to uncover the true cause, and follow wherever a thread of information leads you. Pay attention to your dreams for hidden clues and resonances with other times and events.

Raphael asks:
What are your dreams telling you?

Gloriana's Blessing

My blessing is that you remember the history of your life—however long or short it has been so far—and that you can see the strands of chance and fate that have guided you and continue to influence the road ahead.

Red Historian

JOHN DEE

Oracle of the West

(LOVE/INSPIRATION)

Often the twists and turns of history can be brought about by the smallest and simplest event. In life and love the same truth obtains. Be aware of small but significant events, and if you are actively searching for love, remember that it requires reciprocation. Consider also that whatever most inspires you can change without warning, and it is wise to be prepared for that possibility.

Gabriel asks:
What are the key events in your life right now?

Dee's passion for history marks him out as the Red Historian. Throughout his life he maintained a fascination with the earliest history of Britain and wrote about it a number of times. He seems to have made little distinction between fact and legend, but the wisdom he derived from his studies was unaffected by this. Because he believed implicitly that everything was connected, he saw history as a series of mirrors held up to humankind in which they might perceive lessons and truths that could help them both in present and future times. In the *Oracle* he helps us find our sense of inner purpose and direction.

Oracle of the North

(WORK/LIVING)

Don't get too bogged down in the minutiae of living, since this is simply a distraction. The great events of your life will stand out, as do the turning points of history. Consider the shape of your life to date and see if this suggests new directions ahead. If you feel stuck or listless, it may be time for a change. Even the smallest alteration can bring relief in all kinds of ways.

Uriel asks:
What changes do you think you might need to make?

Oracle of the Centre

(GENERAL/PERSONAL)

Your true purpose may be different from what you think. Often, people are led to follow a direction that, despite the apparent satisfaction it brings, is not what they truly wish to do. Consider alternatives, even if this results in upheaval. Face the reality of your inner destiny and follow it as committedly as you can.

Oracle of the East

(HEALTH/WELL-BEING)

The getting of wisdom can also bring suffering, especially in the area of health. You may feel that anything is worth the gain of understanding and enlightenment, but be careful not to rush in without considering all the possibilities available to you. Tune yourself to the brilliance of the world around you, and you will find your own life brightened as a result.

Raphael asks:
What is the greatest source of joy in your life?

Oracle of the South

(INTENTION/DIRECTION)

Whatever rules your life most strongly should always be kept fresh and alive. Neglecting the inner compass that guides you can spell disaster. Renew your vows to yourself and the inner vision that drives you as often as you can, for nothing is wholly constant and unchanging. Focus on your deepest resources and keep them bright.

Michael asks:
How can you best care for your inner life?

Gloriana's Blessing

My blessing is that you are able to understand the tides that shape your life. None are irreversible, but properly acknowledged, they can and will usher you into fresh waters.

Gold Historian

RAPHAEL HOLINSHED

Oracle of the West

(LOVE/INSPIRATION)

Is it affection or fear of being alone that drives your relationships with those around you? Remember that you may well be a mirror to others just as often as they are to you. Consider what truly motivates the face and character you present to the world, asking yourself what aspect of your personal history colours it.

Gabriel asks:
What face do you present to the world?

The Gold Historian, Raphael Holinshed (1529–80), created one of the most important books of English chronicles. In 1548 the printer Reginald Wolfe came up with the idea of creating a "Universal Cosmography of the whole world." Quickly realising that he could not complete this project alone, he hired Holinshed to assist him. However, the work was never finished, though one volume was published in 1577 as *The Chronicles of England, Scotland, and Ireland*. This book became the source for most of Shakespeare's history dramas. Holinshed himself remains mysterious. Virtually nothing is known of his life, though he is believed to have been born in Cheshire and to have attended Cambridge University. In the *Oracle* he represents a subtle combining of truth with imagination, and the ability to see a shape within the most random-seeming events.

Oracle of the North

(WORK/LIVING)

If you have moved from job to job more than twice in the past two years or have a habit of switching paths regularly, you might need to consider the underlying reasons for this. What is there in your history that makes you seek change or be dissatisfied with your lot? Sometimes this may point to an eagerness to get ahead, but remember that the strongest structures are built upon solid foundations, not upon sand.

Uriel asks:
What is the true foundation in your life and work?

Oracle of the Centre

(GENERAL/PERSONAL)

In the history of your life are all the clues you need to read the future. No matter how many changes of direction attend you, there is always a reason, a pattern that may be discerned. Look to the significant points in your life, which are not always so easy to see as you think, and search out the significances to be found there. If there are unresolved matters from your past, these may need your attention to clear the way ahead.

Oracle of the South

(INTENTION/DIRECTION)

Recording your aims and ambitions either in writing or speech can bring fresh understanding and awareness to your daily life. It can also point the way forward and help you organise your thoughts. Consider the most-natural-seeming shapes and patterns you seek to implement, and be realistic in your interpretation. Do not pretend you can advance when you very clearly cannot.

Michael asks:
What patterns can you see in your life?

Oracle of the East

(HEALTH/WELL-BEING)

Past traumas can sometimes resurface in the present, causing issues both to health and general life. Consider carefully if there are still unresolved aspects of these earlier events that need your attention. Look for root causes beneath the outer aspects of any illness or dramatic upheavals in your life. Remember that even physical ailments can possess interior causes.

Raphael asks:
Are there unresolved issues you have not dealt with?

Gloriana's Blessing

This is my blessing to you—that the fearful shall no longer attend your waking and dreaming self, and that memories will take their place in the patterns of your life without harm or consequence.

Silver Historian

POLYDORE VIRGIL

Oracle of the West

(LOVE/INSPIRATION)

The history of your life is an ongoing network of events, made mutable by your decisions. Wherever the compass of your soul guides you, take care that you consider every aspect before you embark on a new journey. Learn from your own past history and try to imagine what your future will be like. Signposts may well be hidden, but they are present, nonetheless.

Gabriel asks:

Where is your inner compass guiding you?

Polydore Virgil (ca. 1470–1555), the Silver Historian, was an Italian who became one of the most important chroniclers of the Tudor dynasty. He was hired by Henry VIII to record his life and that of his father, Henry VII. Commissioned to write a history of England, he took almost thirty years to complete the work, which extended to twenty-seven volumes. His book is a monument to his research, which includes works from other countries as well as England. Dee numbered several of his books among his personal collection. Within the *Oracle*, he represents a sober and careful consideration of all facts in a given situation.

Oracle of the North

(WORK/LIVING)

Even the greatest success stories have moments of downturn. Without dwelling too much on possible future events, try to be prepared for all eventualities. The history of your life, however far into it you may be, can still offer good advice to you. Admired individuals, with whom you share aspects of your own life and personality, may also have important messages for you. You can learn a great deal from the example of others.

Uriel asks:
Whom do you most admire as a role model, and why?

Oracle of the Centre

(GENERAL/PERSONAL)

Consider if you are truly aware of both the positive and negative aspects of your life and whether you acknowledge these enough. Try to find a point of balance in all things and do not be afraid of past mistakes repeating themselves without reason. If you tend to rush into things without thinking, try to consider as much as you can what the long-term results may be.

Oracle of the South

(INTENTION/DIRECTION)

The sense of direction that guides you every day can be disrupted by powerful and unexpected events. Bring yourself back to your goal by focusing on the bigger picture. Support may come from the most unlikely sources, and no offer of help should be refused without good reason. Be purposeful, but remember there will always be moments of uncertainty.

Michael asks:
How aware are you of your inner compass?

Oracle of the East

(HEALTH/WELL-BEING)

The body is an index of the many things that have happened to it—including illness and the adventures of daily living. The more in touch you are with yourself, the more you will understand. Look for the signs. Remember the history of your physical life. Be alert to the truth that memories can offer.

Raphael asks:
What is your physical self telling you now?

Gloriana's Blessing

For you, I invoke this blessing: that you may learn the lessons of history, that you do not dismiss the past as without value, and that, with the guidance of the Ancestors, you find your way to your Long Home.

The Changing Card

GLORIANA

Elizabeth I (1533–1603) is perhaps the greatest and most famous monarch to rule over England. She was the daughter of Henry VIII and Anne Boleyn, and her reign lasted from November 1558 until her death in 1603. During this time, she led the country against an attempted invasion by the Spanish king Philip II in 1588 (the famous Spanish Armada) and established a court filled with notable figures. Many pursued her with amorous intent but found her resistant to marriage, earning her the title "the Virgin Queen." In the latter part of her life, a personality cult grew around her, and she became a central figure in several great works of literature, such as *The Faerie Queene* by Edmund Spenser, one of the first to call her "Gloriana."

To many of her subjects, Elizabeth became an almost mythical figure, admired and sometimes even worshipped as more than mortal. The many portraits that still exist depict her in increasingly magical and mythological forms, which is reflected in our version, based on the so-called "Rainbow" portrait. Her reign saw an extraordinary flourishing of English drama and literature, with playwrights such as William Shakespeare and Christopher Marlowe, and poets such as Philip Sidney and Michael Drayton. At the same time, she encouraged the search for new lands to bring under her banner, with famous explorers such as Sir Francis Drake and Sir Walter Raleigh leading the way in the discovery and colonization of the Americas.

We have titled this extra card *The Changing Card*, bearing in mind that reigning monarchs have long held the power to reverse rulings, such as orders of execution and possession of lands. In the *Oracle*, this card represents Queen Elizabeth as Gloriana. It has the power to reverse a reading and can be used as such when it appears in a spread. If the Queen appears on any of the Towers in the layout following Dee's design for *The Golden Talisman*, especially in the central position of Harmony, she offers the option to reverse the meaning of that position. The decision to do so rests with the reader. Even if the card does not appear in the random selection, her blessings are present on each card and should be included in the interpretation of the reading.

The Hieroglyphic Monad

CARD BACK

This curious and complex symbol, which appears on the backs of the cards, was devised by Dee himself in 1564. It embodied Dee's vision of the unity of the cosmos and is a composite of various esoteric and astrological symbols. From top to bottom, it represented the moon, the sun, and the elements. Dee's own commentary is extremely obscure, but it is clear that he saw the Monad as a key both to his own work and the universal code that he sought throughout his life. In the *Oracle*, it stands for the coming together of the elements and the harmonious conclusion of every reading undertaken.

• PART FOUR •

Working with the Oracle

There is a body of a body
And a soul and a Spirit
Within two bodies must be knit.

There be two earths as I tell
And two waters with them to dwell.
The one is white the other red—
The quick, and the bodies that be dead.

And one fire in nature hid
And one air which them doth abide
And all it cometh out of one kind.
Mark this well man in thy mind.

(NOTEBOOKS OF JOHN DEE, 1589)

~ A SAMPLE READING ~

Here are some practical suggestions for extending your work with *The John Dee Oracle*, beginning with a reading made for a client using the deck. This example illustrates the kind of question asked and the form the answer might take.

Stephen had reached a well-established position in middle management at a prestigious workplace, but he was feeling increasingly under pressure and uncertain about the best path to follow. He was considering taking an extended holiday to give himself time to reflect on his options, the direction of his career, and how his plans to propose to his long-time fiancée might affect this. He sought a general overview of his life from the *Oracle*.

Stephen drew five cards, placing the first, *The Silver Astronomer*, at the central point (Harmony). The *Oracle*'s message for this card in that position conveyed the following:

ORACLE OF THE CENTRE: SILVER ASTRONOMER (PERSONAL/GENERAL)

If you are a determined person but easily distracted, you may be tempted to make wrong decisions if the outcome appears attractive. Look deeper until you are certain of the most-likely effects of your choice. Review your life plan. You may feel unusually tired and lacking motivation, but if you allow yourself to look beyond surface appearances, you will discover new reserves of energy and fresh motivation.

Stephen accepted that this was an accurate description of both his character and current situation, though he was uncertain of any spiritual aspect in his life. Before moving on to the four cards at the Tower positions, Stephen invoked **Gloriana's Blessing** for the **Silver Astronomer**:

The blessing I offer is that you find stability to withstand the daily challenges that life ushers in. Remember to look to those closest to you for support and acknowledge the welcome respite of kindness.

This gave Stephen a sense of hope and reassurance. He then turned his attention to ***Septentrio*** in the North.

SEPTENTRIO ORACLE OF THE NORTH: GREEN PHYSICIAN

If work is becoming too much for you, try to stay in a relaxed frame of mind and make time to take regular breaks. Even five minutes sitting in a chair and breathing evenly, or taking a brisk walk around the block, can restore flagging energies and will more than repay the time taken.

Again, the **Blessing from the Queen** was to the point:

My blessing to you is that you are aware of the truth underlying all that occurs, that you do not lose your way in the many turning points of your life, and that you find healing whenever it is required.

ORIENS
ORACLE OF THE EAST: SILVER GEOGRAPHER

There are times when strength may fail you, when to even put one foot in front of the other may become difficult. This can be a health issue, or something deeper. It can be the cause of depression or simply lethargy. You should fight against this with every fibre of your being. Do not confuse this experience with simple exhaustion or the need for a rest. Keep awake to the options offered to you, seek progress by easy stages, but never let your chances slip away though lack of concentration and energy.

The Blessing for the **Silver Geographer** was

I offer you the blessing of honesty, the ability to see beyond the surface of your issues, and the strength to ride out the harshest periods of your life until you emerge into fresh morning light.

MERIDIENS
ORACLE OF THE SOUTH: GOLD ALCHEMIST

No matter how familiar a road may seem, you can still get lost. Always watch for signposts and stay alert to the messages they offer. These signs are often not obvious at first glance, so observe carefully. The broadest way may not always be the right one for you; consider the less trodden path if it feels right. Wherever your path leads, be willing to accept help and advice when it is well intentioned.

Gloriana's blessing was as apposite as ever:

The blessing I give is one of self-awareness. Allow every moment that passes to be filled with strength and joy. Remember who you are and what gifts you possess.

OCCIDENS
ORACLE OF THE WEST: SILVER HISTORIAN

The history of your life is an ongoing network of events, made mutable by your decisions. Wherever the compass of your soul guides you, take care that you consider every aspect before you embark on a new journey. Learn from your own past history and try to imagine what your future will be like. Signposts may well be hidden, but they are present, nonetheless.

The **Queen's Blessing** for this card was especially good and gave Stephen much food for thought:

> *For you, I invoke this blessing: that you may learn the lessons of history, that you do not dismiss the past as without value, and that, with the guidance of the Ancestors, you find your way to your Long Home.*

Stephen considered all the meanings and blessings he had received from the *Oracle* and decided that the balance suggested he should undertake the journey he was planning, but with careful consideration of all options beforehand. He also recognized that the uncertainty he had been experiencing was beginning to hold him back from moving forward altogether. Gloriana's blessings were particularly empowering, pointing to a successful outcome if he could overcome his doubts and follow the path ahead without fear.

Under the circumstances, Stephen moderated his plans. Instead of taking a month off, he decided on a two-week break. During this time, he proposed to his fiancée, who accepted. Upon returning from his holiday, Stephen discovered he was in line for a promotion, which he would have missed out on had he taken a longer time away. However, the time off and the blossoming of his personal life led him to consult the *Oracle* further. As a result, he chose to change the direction of his life, settling for a less pressured job in the countryside, where he could raise a family.

~ THE ANCIENT ART OF SCRYING ~

Much of the information acquired by Dee and Kelly came to them through scrying, an ancient method of receiving spiritual visions or seeking clues to help answer questions and resolve issues in daily life. *The John Dee Oracle* works in a similar way, guiding users to discover advice and solutions to their problems. In this case, we have replaced the traditional crystal ball or scrying mirror with cards that draw upon the collective wisdom of Dee, Kelly, and some of the greatest minds of the Renaissance. However, the ancient art of scrying remains valid and can still offer remarkably effective solutions.

Traditionally, scrying involved using either a crystal ball or a reflective surface, such as a mirror or polished object. These tools are still available today, with polished black mirrors, often made of obsidian, being readily accessible. Another simple method of scrying was practised by Nostradamus, a renowned seer of roughly the same period as Dee. He even documented the method he used, which can easily be employed today.

Nostradamus described sitting alone in his study, lit only by a flickering candle, bent over a bowl of water. Sometimes, he added pungent oils and breathed them in while focusing on the images in the water's depths. He wrote, "*I emptied my soul, brain, and heart of all care and attained a state of tranquility and stillness of mind, which are prerequisites for predicting.*"

This method is easily accessible to anyone. Find a quiet place where you won't be disturbed, and don't forget to turn off your phone! Darken the room as much as possible and light a candle, positioning it where you can observe any changes in the flame. Take a deep bowl, preferably with a plain, dark interior, and fill it halfway with water. You may wish to add scented oil to aid concentration. Sit over the bowl, allowing your mind to relax, and stare into the depths with slightly unfocused eyes until you begin to see or sense images. You might choose to stir the water gently by moving the bowl, or by dropping small pebbles into it to create movement, but equally, still water can reveal much. Observe the patterns that form and take note of how the candlelight changes or how it reflects in the water.

Interpreting what you see is personal and intuitive, but with time and practice, you may be surprised by how much you can discover within the water.

If you choose to use a crystal ball, the process is similarly simple. Place the ball on a piece of dark cloth (black is traditional) and set up a candle or another soft light source nearby, but not shining directly at you or the crystal. Relax your sight and calm your mind—this can take time, especially if you're not used to meditating—then look for shapes and patterns within the crystal. You might find it helpful to describe out loud what you see, since this distracts the busy conscious mind and allows you to focus more deeply on the random images that arise. Avoid forcing the interpretation; instead, let ideas and thoughts surface naturally.

If you wish to try scrying with the cards from *The John Dee Oracle*, you can lay out several cards in a row (the number is up to you, but we suggest a small, random selection). Place a light beside you and, as previously described, clear your mind, steady your breathing, and allow your conscious focus to soften. Let the cards speak to you. Each of the great figures depicted on the cards may have a personal message for you. This method differs from a traditional reading, which involves laying out the cards in a specific pattern and using the interpretations provided in the book. Instead, it offers greater freedom, allowing the unconscious mind to reveal aspects of a problem or situation that you might not have been aware of.

In all cases, write down or record what you see or hear for future reference.

~ MEDITATION: A VISIT WITH DR DEE ~

The following meditation is intended to give the user of the *Oracle* a direct experience of Dr Dee. Follow your preferred method of meditation, or by breathing and allowing the stresses and strains of the day to dissolve. Close your eyes and breathe deeply, then open them and read the text slowly and carefully. If you find yourself drifting off, follow the path and see where it leads:

As you allow your present surroundings to fade, see before you a wooden door, the entrance to John Dee's house in Mortlake, London. It opens at your touch, revealing a stair, curving upward into shadow. You set your feet upon the stair and begin to climb . . .

Soon you emerge into a small circular chamber at the top of the house. A fire burns brightly in a small hearth, and the only other source of light is a tall candle in a sconce and a few fitful rays of sunlight entering through a small leaded window . . .

Before you, taking up much of the space in the chamber, is a large desk, cluttered with papers, an astrolabe, compasses, glass vials and retorts, and the many tools of a working astrologer and alchemist. To one side, a small telescope sits on a tripod, its lens aimed at the window . . .

Behind the desk sits a figure you recognise at once as John Dee. He is bent over a roll of parchment, on which he is writing lines of numbers and letters. Becoming aware of you, he raises his head and indicates that you should be seated in the only other chair in the room, on the nearside of the desk . . .

Staring at you intensely, he asks why you have come. You make your response according to your personal feelings. Perhaps you have come to ask for a reading, a horoscope, or simply some advice . . .

Having heard your words, Dr Dee indicates a circular object covered by a black cloth on the desk before him. He lifts the cover to reveal a shining obsidian mirror—his famous scrying glass. Dee invites you to look into this. Bending over it, you stare deeply into the pool of darkness until shapes and images, maybe words, begin to float there. Look carefully and try to remember all that you see . . .

After a time, you pull yourself back from the mirror and address Dr Dee, telling him as fully as you can what you saw . . .

Dee responds, perhaps interpreting the images or words you saw, or simply suggesting ways these might reflect a situation in your life. Take time to listen . . .

When you have heard all that Dr Dee has to tell you, take your leave of him and return by way of the downward-curving stair, though the wooden door, and back into your everyday consciousness. Write down all that you can remember of the journey and the words spoken to you by Dr John Dee.

~ THE ENOCHIAN ALPHABET AND ITS POWERS ~

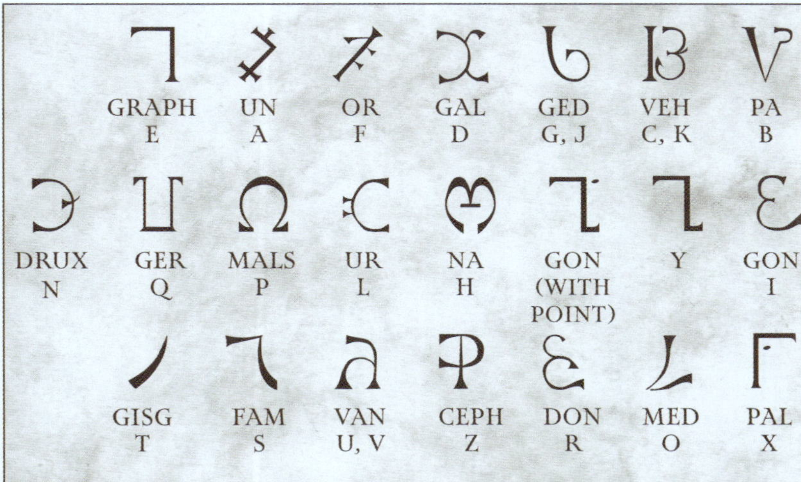

THE LETTERS READ HERE FROM RIGHT TO LEFT, AS WRITTEN IN DEE'S DIARY.

The mysterious alphabet received by Dee and Kelly from angelic sources is at the heart of all their magical work from 1583 onward. Much has been written about this by practitioners of the magical arts, but little is understood to this day. A number of short verses, which Dee termed "Calls" or "Angelic Keys," were published in 1584. He indicated that these contained a means of interpreting the letters, though they are really invocations of the angelic powers. Translation is difficult and highly speculative, but we include a selection of these here in case the user of *The John Dee Oracle* might like to add these to the interpretation of their reading. The translations are our own and are freely interpreted. Not all the calls—there are nineteen in all—are appropriate here, but we quickly noticed that some were oriented toward the four directions. Given that the original Golden Talisman is also designed around the four cardinal points, and that this was the principle upon which the *Oracle* is based, we decided to include these four calls here, along with the two that seemed most appropriate to the Centre, and from which you can chose the one that seems most fitting. If you decide to use these, we suggest they be applied to the directions as adjuncts to the readings you make from the cards, and that you speak them aloud before studying your reading.

THE SECOND CALL (THE CENTRE)

Can the winds interpret your wondering voices?
You who were not at the beginning,
That fire has kept within my mouth
Whom I have prepared as a wedding cup
Or flowers for the bridal chamber.
You are stronger than stone
And your voices are louder than the winds;
You have become as a building
Which lives only in the mind of the Creator.
Arise, he says, and show yourselves,
Seethe with the power you possess—
For I am He that lives forever.

THE THIRD CALL (THE CENTRE)

Behold, I am a circle upon which
Stands twelve kingdoms.
Six are the seats of the living breath,
The rest are sharper than death
And within them, the creatures of the earth
Are and are not; sleep and arise.
I made you stewards and set you
In seats of government,
Giving you power to rule
Over true ages of time,
So that you might work my power,
Pouring the fires of life and increase
Constantly upon the earth.
You are the skirts of justice and truth
And in God's name should lift yourselves up.
Behold His mighty name;
Move, descend, and apply yourselves
To the secret wisdom of Creation.

THE FOURTH CALL (SOUTH)

My feet are in the South
Where thunders increase
Under them I have placed
Those who understand great numbers,
Who are second to none

And grow ever stronger.
Arise, you sons of pleasure,
Visit the earth,
For I am the Lord.
In the Creator's name
Move, show yourselves
Be as deliverers unto men.

THE SEVENTH CALL (EAST)

The East is a virgin place,
Where praises are sung
Amid the first glorious flames
That issued from the mouth of the Lord.
Now there are twenty-eight houses
In which men rejoice.
They are clad in bright ornaments,
They are amazing to all creatures,
They are strong towers of comfort,
Seats of mercy and constancy.
O you servants of mercy,
Move, appear, sing to the Creator,
Dwell amongst us. For thus does
Remembrance, power and strength
Wax strong, to our comfort.

THE NINTH CALL (WEST)

Mighty guardians of fire
Each with a two-edged sword,
With wings of wormwood
And marrow of salt,
Have settled in the West.
They gather up mosses
As the rich man gathers his treasure
In their eyes are millstones
And from their mouths comes blood;
Their heads are covered with diamonds
And on their arms are sleeves of stone.
Happy is the one on whom
They do not look askance,
For thus God rejoices.
Come, for this is a time
That requires comfort.

THE TENTH CALL (NORTH)

A thunder of judgement
Is harboured by the North,
In the likeness of an oak
In whose branches are nests
Of sorrow and weeping,
Laid up for the earth.
They burn night and day
And give forth scorpions
And poisonous sulphur.
These thunders never rest
and know nothing of time.
Here, a single stone
Can bring forth a thousand,
Even as does the heart of man
Bring forth thoughts
To trouble the earth.
Come—but leave behind your voices.

§§§

Thus we reach the end of the beginning of the work with *The John Dee Oracle*. It is our hope that it will offer wisdom and insight both in your daily concerns and your general advancement through life in its most spiritual dimension. We leave you with a last, general blessing from *Gloriana* herself:

To all who open the ways between the worlds

and cross the boundaries of time with this Oracle,

I send my blessing that you shall find the heart of all you seek for whatever reason you are journeying.

Further Reading

There are many fine books on John Dee available today. Here are some of the ones we found most useful:

Casaubon, Meric. *A True and Faithful Relation of What Passed for Many Years Between Dr. John Dee and Some Spirits*. 1659. Reprinted frequently, including a facsimile by Golden Dragon, n.d.

Cresswell, Julia. *The Watkins Dictionary of Angels*. London: Watkins, 2006.

Dakin, Nicholas. *John Dee of Mortlake*. Barnes, UK: Mortlake History Society, 2011.

French, Peter J. *John Dee: The World of an Elizabethan Magus*. London: RKP, 1972.

Klein, Kevin. *The Complete Mystical Records of Dr. John Dee (3-Volume Set): Transcribed from the 16th-Century Manuscripts Documenting Dee's Conversations with Angels*. Woodbury, MN: Llewellyn, 2020.
(The best and most comprehensible collection of Dee's writings to date)

Laycock, Donald C. *The Complete Enochian Dictionary*. York Beach, ME: Weiser Books, 2001.

Parry, Glyn. *The Arch-Conjuror of England: John Dee*. New Haven, CT: Yale University Press, 2011.

Woolley, Benjamin. *The Queen's Conjuror: The Science and Magic of Dr. John Dee, Adviser to Queen Elizabeth I*. London: HarperCollins, 2001.

About the Authors

John Matthews has produced a number of successful divinatory systems based on early spiritual beliefs—including the *Arthurian Tarot* (with Caitlín Matthews and Miranda Gray), the bestselling *Wildwood Tarot* (with Mark Ryan and Will Worthington), and *The Lost Tarot of Nostradamus* (with Wil Kinghan). He is widely known as the author of numerous books on the Grail and Arthurian legends, as well as volumes of Celtic literature, myth, and belief. His book *Pirates* was a No. 1 *New York Times* bestseller for twenty-two weeks in 2007. Matthews has served as an advisor on several motion pictures, including Jerry Bruckheimer's *King Arthur*, and is currently involved in a number of film projects of his own. He also appeared in the TV documentary series *Nostradamus: End of Days* (Discovery+, 2021).

Wil Kinghan is a writer, artist, and explorer of Celtic traditions. He studied archaeology at University College Dublin and environmental design at NCAD before working in advertising and commercial television as an art director, where he won awards for various campaigns. As a writer, Wil is a published poet, with *Where the Hazel Falls* (Electric Publications) to his name, as well as coauthor of *The Shaman's Oracle* (with John Matthews), *The Celtic Wisdom Oracle* (with Caitlín Matthews), and *The Steampunk Tarot* (with John and Caitlín Matthews). He is currently working on his first novel, *Werewolves*, and developing several feature films and TV programmes. Wil lives in Oxford with his wife, Melanie, their daughter, Annabelle, and their son, Leo.